SMOKY MOUNTAIN HIGH

The Consuming Passion
of Cecil Brown

By Frank Duracher

Salvation Army National Publications
615 Slaters Lane
Alexandria, Virginia 22313

Published by Crest Books
The Salvation Army National Headquarters
615 Slaters Lane, Alexandria, VA 22313
Major Ed Forster, Editor in Chief for National Publications and National Literary
Secretary
Phone: 703/684-5523
Fax: 703/302-8617

Available from The Salvation Army Supplies and Purchasing Departments
  Des Plaines, IL – (800) 937-8896
  West Nyack, NY – (888) 488-4882
  Atlanta, GA – (800) 786-7372
  Long Beach, CA – (800) 937-8896

Printed in the United States of America

Library of Congress Control Number: 2007927724

Photos courtesy of Major Frank Duracher, the Asheville, N.C., *Citizen Times*, and the
National Headquarters Archives and Research Center

Editorial Assistant, Judith L. Brown
Original art work by D. Morgan (Doris Whitten Morgan)
Design by Henry Cao

ISBN–10: 0-9792266-1-9
ISBN–13: 978-09792266-1-8

Contents

Dedication

To Major Janet Elizabeth Duracher,
who encouraged and prodded me
throughout the process of writing this book,

and

to Major Margery Ann Duracher,
who would have – but the Lord called her Home.

Foreword

Major Cecil Brown was an extraordinary officer and a legendary figure of The Salvation Army in the Southern Territory, USA. A daughter of the remote mountain culture of North Carolina in the early part of the twentieth century, she became an apostle to her own people. Having become a Salvationist while visiting her brother in Asheville, she became an officer shortly thereafter. As a young officer, she soon felt the pull to bring the hope of the gospel and the compassion of Christ to the unchurched and impoverished families of her beloved mountains. Her divisional commander agreed to allow her to give this bold mission a try. And the rest, as they say, is history.

We owe Frank Duracher a debt of gratitude for his painstaking research in gathering the information and interviewing people who knew Cecil Brown or worked alongside her. The fruit of his labor and insight is found in the pages you are about to read. The writer has done well in describing both the context (mountain culture) and the content (ministry) of Cecil Brown's mountain mission. He has also given us insight into the person so as to help us understand the character and commitment that enabled her to do the seemingly impossible.

Every missional Salvationist of our day can learn from Cecil Brown. She felt God's call to a very clearly defined mission. It became her focus – indeed, her obsession – for the rest of her life. She faced and overcame numerous formidable obstacles in her pursuit of that calling. She disciplined her days, hours, and minutes by it. She gathered around her helpers of like mind. She recognized ability and reliability and commissioned ordinary people to mission tasks.

Perhaps her greatest attribute – and the primary reason for her mission effectiveness – was the incarnational character of her shepherding. She took on the "flesh and blood" of mountain life and culture. She shared their suffering, understood their pain, became the compassion of God in their lives, expended herself for them, advocated on their behalf, taught them Christian values, and led many to Christ and to discipleship. She became a trusted spiritual guide for their journey through life – a shepherdess.

Again and again, those who had known her spoke of her decisive influence on their own lives and the lives of many others. She possessed a strong will which sometimes led to confrontation but without which the Mountain Mission would never have succeeded. Like William Booth she was impatient with those who doubted her vision, tried to contain her leadership, or resented the discipline she expected of her co-workers. But also like the Army's Founder, her compassion for a world that needed Christ (in her case, the mountain people of western North Carolina) was the real driving force that won the hearts of her widespread mountain flock and the respect of thousands.

The Shepherdess of the Hills was a model of mission leadership. She had a passion for mission combined with persistence to follow it. She was clear about the people grouping to which she was called to bring the gospel. She did not allow obstacles of any kind to deter her. She used the leadership strengths she had and enlisted others to do what she couldn't. She was there for her people when they needed her.

She respected their culture and adapted worship and teaching to it. She organized her mission so that it endured until most of the people and their descendents had left the remote mountain areas. It was a strategy that worked, probably the only strategy that *could* have worked. I suspect it is a strategy that succeeds on just about any mission field.

Commissioner Phil Needham (Retired)
Former Southern USA Territorial Commander
The Salvation Army

Acknowledgments

Some material for this book is based on an unfinished manuscript written by Lt. Colonel Wesley Bouterse in the 1940's. His work covered the first few years of Cecil's ministry in the mountains. The author wishes to acknowledge his indebtedness to this earlier research and work by Colonel Bouterse. We also have used newspaper and *War Cry* clippings.

Beyond that, we have the first-hand accounts of the women who assisted her, others who knew her, and the recollections of several of her relatives. Some of these interviews are particularly significant. The list of contributors includes: Major Glenna West, Major Florence (Wall) Brewer, Brigadier James Henry, Brigadier Dorothy Langston, Major Mildred (Kirby) Foden, Major Jean Frese, Major Doris McQuay, Dean (Self) Silvers, June (Brown) Ferguson, CSM Wayne Moore, Fanny (Rathbone) Ledford, Blanche (Lowe) Wimbish, Thelma (Hall) Askew, Troy Self, Major Sam Bivans, Brigadier Ivy Waterworth, Brigadier Katherine Millsap, and Brigadier Evelyn Sams.

Many thanks to others who helped with editing, critiquing and research: Commissioner Philip Needham, Colonel Henry Gariepy, Colonel Marjorie Gariepy, Lt. Colonel Marlene Chase, Major Carolyn Gesner, Major Allen Satterlee, Dan Childs, Judith Brown and Major Ed Forster. Thanks above all to my wife, Major Elizabeth Duracher, who sifted through countless materials and articles. She also helped with proofreading and setting up many interviews and on-site research expeditions. By coincidence, early in her officership, as Lieutenant Elizabeth Fowler she served for a year as corps officer at Shelton Laurel. This gave her the opportunity to add her own perspective of having pastored in the Mountain Mission as a part of Cecil Brown's team. In fact, some of the furniture pieces in Libby's quarters consisted of items made by Cecil's brothers.

Today the Mountain Mission, coordinated in nearby Waynesville, North Carolina, comprises the four highest-altitude corps in the USA Southern Territory. Although the present day work resembles little of the rustic and romantic ambience so dominant when Cecil trekked these hills, the motivation for service remains the same.

Times change – so do people and their needs. Even in retirement, Cecil Brown considered her work unfinished. She spoke of hating to leave her work behind, but she also looked forward to seeing her Savior face-to-face.

She once wrote, "(I find) in each testimony of God's past and present blessings, there comes almost daily the call of outstretched hands in new fields, and thus the future stretching out into an ever-widening horizon."

Introduction

Maple Springs, Little Creek, Shelton Laurel, White Oak, Bonnie Hill, Cold Springs, Max Patch and Fines Creek are names of remote North Carolina hamlets tucked into the region along the eastern border of the Great Smoky Mountains National Park.

This is the story of a determined young mountain girl who fell in love with the mission of the Salvation Army and wanted to lift her own people to new heights. Daisy Cecil Brown left the mountains to find her destiny. As a Salvation Army officer, she served in a handful of appointments during her career. But the one appointment that mattered most turned out to be her last, and it was more than 20 years in the making. She returned to the mountains to fulfill her destiny, which she believed was truly the will of God. A few common threads are evident in this story.

The work of the Salvation Army might not have taken root without Cecil Brown. She represents the rare leader who could have pulled off such a mammoth effort. Had she not stepped forward to fulfill this destiny, God certainly could have raised up someone else to do it. But she made herself available, and the Lord didn't have to look any further than the hamlet of Hurricane Creek.

Consciously or not, Cecil used her disadvantages – her gender, her lack of education, and her indigenous roots – to her decided advantage. With those "advantages" the Army's work in these mountains took hold. Although the mountaineers distrusted outsiders, they accepted her because she was one of them. They may have come to listen to her out of curiosity or courtesy, but they came. Many of them stayed and joined the Army.

Most people who knew her had strong opinions about her. There was very little middle ground. One of her former assistants loves and respects her so deeply that she hopes to build a museum at Shelton Laurel to display her collection of mission artifacts. Another former assistant confessed to harboring so much hurt during the three years she spent with Cecil, that even 50 years later she still asks God to forgive her anger.

Some interviewees would not go on record about certain facts. Many times, an interviewee might say something like, "Turn that tape recorder off and I will tell you!" In those instances, the information was unusable. Some stories offered a different version of the same incident.

Cecil Brown was probably what we would call today a workaholic. She was stern, but she was usually viewed as fair. Most people considered her willing to do everything she asked her assistant officers and soldiers to do. Some people think she pushed herself into an early grave. It is unclear as to when she was diagnosed with the cancer that eventually took her life. Was it *before* her retirement? Was the retirement *because of* her sickness? Was her sickness the reason why some people believed her behavior in the last years of her life to be more temperamental?

Cecil's vision was to lift her people to a higher level – spiritually, socially and even culturally – while still retaining their Appalachian uniqueness. That is why this biography is titled *Smoky Mountain High: The Consuming Passion of Cecil Brown.*

Major Brown knew each hamlet and its people well. As a young woman she met the Army while visiting her brother in Asheville, N.C. She attended the corps, enrolled as a soldier and was recognized by Captain Dorothy Guice, her corps officer, as having potential. Soon Cecil was off to the training college in Atlanta, Georgia.

After commissioning and appointments to several corps, the lure to her native roots became a growing passion. She envisioned a work among her people with a central community house and branch missions wherever they were needed.

Finally, in 1935, she received an appointment to the land she loved so that she could minister to hundreds of unchurched families. In a later *War Cry* interview, she sounded overjoyed in her reaction to the good news. "In my heart was a burning for the people who were still as I had been, and finally came the day – the door was open at last," she said.

At first Cecil did most of her on-site work in rustic log cabins. Some mission stations, such as Cold Creek and Big Bend, were lumber camps that evaporated when the timber was finally used up. The mission included a school and a shelter for children; craft rooms where women learned to weave rugs, towels and other household articles; and a trading post store where those items were sold to support the mission. Every corps faithfully conducted mission activities at each outpost. One meeting place was located in a hayloft!

First on foot, then on horseback, and finally by jeep, Cecil founded a ministry that still exists today. She was a latter-day circuit rider traversing narrow mountain trails, swelling creeks and muddy roads until her retirement in 1956. Often while traveling her circuit, she stopped to preach wherever there was a crowd.

Besides her pastoral duties, which included everything from prayers to prescriptions, the "Maid of the Mountains" provided food, clothing and material necessities to the remotest of families. Each December she became a "Lady Santa Claus," organizing twelve Christmas parties and providing gifts and necessities for hundreds of isolated mountain families.

She began the annual "Singing on the Mountain," also called "The Singing Convention," which was a daylong concert in the open-air featuring soloists and groups from across the country. This event continued to attract gospel music lovers until 2003.

Most of the people who assisted Major Brown agree that she was stern and deeply focused, but that she had a tender heart for her people. Her burning desire was to serve Christ by ministering to people who needed her help. Many called her the "Shepherdess of the Hills."

For her brilliant service to God, and the mountain people she so loved, in 1947 Major Cecil Brown was admitted to the Order of the Founder, the first person so honored in the USA Southern Territory. About the time of her retirement, she was diagnosed with terminal cancer. She was promoted to Glory at the young age of 51, and she was buried among her beloved hills in Hurricane Valley Cemetery.

Given her efficient nature, everything about her funeral had been planned in advance. She carefully detailed even the particulars about her grave and her headstone. In tribute to the ministry that spanned three decades, merchants in downtown Waynesville placed her photo in newspapers and in their storefronts.

Chapter 1

"You've Got Four Months"

"Captain Brown, I'm going to give you four months to see what you can do with a mission for the people in the mountains." These words, spoken by Salvation Army Major William Gilks, fulfilled a dream.

Here it was – the unmistakable work of God. Captain Daisy Cecil Brown sat silently for a moment to allow the full significance of these unforgettable words to sink in. Four months! It was January 1935, and she would have until late spring to create a viable ministry among her own people. This was a moment she had long envisioned, and it was the realization of her mother's long and earnest prayers!

Maggie Brown had never ceased praying that organized religion would come to her family and friends in the Great Smoky Mountains of western North Carolina. She knew intimately the desperate need of neighboring families for a place to worship God.

"Oh Lord," she cried, "send *someone* who cares to these isolated homes where children are growing up without you, and without help!" But the years passed – Cecil and her siblings grew to adulthood, and still there was no answer from God. With her children gone and retirement approaching, she and her husband Joseph moved from their home in Hurricane Creek, N.C., to Lake Junaluska, N.C., where they could spend their senior years more leisurely.

Surprisingly, Maggie's answer finally came when Cecil returned home on furlough. "Mother," she announced, "the next time I go back to the mountains, I'm going to stay. My next appointment is right there." The irony was not lost on Mrs. Brown – it was strange and marvelous that the Lord would use her own daughter to fulfill her longstanding prayer!

As a novice officer in Salisbury, N.C., Cecil (she preferred her middle name because she thought it sounded more professional than Daisy) had served under Major Gilks, who headed her division. She found her work satisfying and agreed to go wherever the Army sent her, but her heart belonged to the neglected mountain regions of the state.

On one hand, Cecil realized her inadequacies as a Salvation Army officer. She had struggled in the training college, where she often spread her books and notes across her bed and while on her knees prayed for the wherewithal to pass her studies. If she were an applicant to the officer training college today, she might well be refused. She had completed only the seventh grade and then later she finished two semesters of high school.

Nevertheless, Cecil saw a rare chance to try an experiment in a part of the United States that had not been exposed to organized religion. In the high altitudes and remote hollows of western North Carolina, where most residents were upright, God-fearing people, the only spiritual leadership came from sporadic circuit riders. By the time Cecil reached adulthood, even the circuit riders had disappeared, the log cabin churches stood empty, and the people felt as abandoned as sheep without a shepherd.

Cecil was a hard worker, plain in speech and strong in leadership. She spoke the language of the mountain people with an Elizabethan twang, and she knew they would listen to her if she only had the chance! She had prayed and agonized over this beckoning for some time.

When Major Gilk's father, retired Colonel Roy Gilks, visited the Salisbury corps, Cecil seized the moment to explain simply and earnestly her idea for a new and innovative mountain ministry.

Colonel Gilks had a wide range of experience in the British Territory. With the wisdom he had gleaned from years of Army service, the colonel later commented to his son, "Well, *there* is an unusual girl. You ought to give her a chance to do something for her people in the mountains!"

Prudently weighing Cecil's new idea, Major Gilks took care to discern between the romantic visions of a young, enthusiastic officer and the divine calling for an unusual kind of service. Cecil could scarcely believe her ears when she was called to Charlotte and finally given the appointment she had longed for.

On January 31, 1935, Captain Cecil Brown, who had just turned 28 years old, arrived in Waynesville. Located about 28 miles from Asheville, Waynesville was the seat of Haywood County and the gateway to the

Great Smoky Mountains. Cecil claimed a 105-mile area as her parish. She moved into a three-room furnished apartment for $10 per month, which offered steam heat, free water, and electricity for 75 cents a month.

The Asheville *Citizen,* then the largest newspaper in western North Carolina, had heard reports that a determined young Salvationist woman was planning to tackle the Herculean task of opening an Army ministry in the vicinity. The following Sunday the paper ran an article featuring Captain Brown and her new mission in the Smokies. Requests started to pour in from country people on back roads seeking visits from the new "lady preacher."

Each week Cecil dutifully wrote to her divisional commander, informing him of her plans and her progress to date. Her letters during those first few weeks clearly show that she had a sound strategy just waiting to be implemented. Before the first week of her four-month trial period had elapsed, she fretted that deep snow had prevented her from visiting three areas on her itinerary.

In her first letter she wrote, "I have not yet made the round of visits I planned, due to heavy snow, but I am working on three centers. I have been called to one place where there are enough families to have a schoolhouse. The nearest church is five miles away."

Every report to headquarters stressed the inordinate amount of work that stretched before her. She pointed to a widespread need for several mission stations, and she inferred that the four-month trial period should be waived. "There is one high school graduate living in this area. I can make her a Sunday School superintendent. I can preach there once a month, and let her run the Sunday School under my direction. I plan to run the same arrangement at other communities."

"This week I am going ten miles out of Waynesville to a very badly neglected community. There are about 100 children scattered throughout that section that I could get to a Sunday School. Saturday, I went to a big lumber company and found about 100 families living there with no church! I may be able to get the lumber company to back my work. It is 30 miles to the nearest filling station."

Cecil used the plans in her report as a template for her entire Salvation Army mountain ministry. *First,* she would choose and appoint single women leaders to lead mission activities under her watchful command. Next, she would identify unchurched groups of families, for example, the lumber mill camp, where Army work could be endorsed in exchange for spiritual guidance for the workers and their families. Step three included a) targeting unchurched families b) locating communities with no organized church and c) identifying and establishing a rapport with groups of people living miles away from the nearest filling station. In her estimation, gas stations represented the most obvious link to the "outside world."

"I hope," her first report concluded, "by February 15 to have all my plans arranged so that I may give you full details. I am very happy, and feel that I am just where the Lord wants me to be. It seems that He has opened up so many ways already, and I am eager to get going full-swing."

On the next Sunday morning, without a meeting of her own, Cecil and her two sisters visited a small country church in a thickly settled community named Fines Creek. The three uniformed lassies entered the tiny chapel as 35 church members robustly sang *What A Friend We Have In Jesus* and a foot-pump organ blared in true pious style.

"As we marched in," Cecil wrote, "the organ stopped, the singing stopped, and the congregation sat there and stared at us as we found our seats. They were petrified. I hope our uniforms will not upset things as we get started. Continue to pray for us."

The uniform of The Salvation Army has a long tradition of upsetting the status quo all over the world. Many people had stared before, though not nearly as kindly as the good and astonished people of Fines Creek. Cecil and her uniformed helpers were destined to turn many lives right side up on the headwaters of Fines Creek and in the hollows of Haywood and Madison counties.

Fortunately, Captain Brown was not alone. She had family members living nearby who freely offered their support. As corps missions sprouted, parishioners also worked alongside her. Still, the years ahead would demand great sacrifice and much hard work. While outwardly optimistic and enthusiastic, inwardly Cecil felt insecure and inadequate for the huge task that was placed before her. She mostly kept her thoughts and feelings to herself, but she vented her occasional depression by writing down her private thoughts in a personal diary.

Her January 23, 1936 diary entry read: "Walked out from Brother Hill's. It was two-below-zero, but I visited some and finally got home before going to my lonely bunk – am all discouraged tonight."

Cecil entering the Training College, circa 1925

Chapter 2

A World Apart

In the late 1700's, Cecil Brown's great grandfather had staked a home-stead of more than 700 acres in Haywood County, N.C. Although a ti-tle challenge narrowed the deed to 100 acres, Cecil's ancestors still had enough fertile acreage left over to farm for an adequate living. Three generations later, they would continue to reap their livelihood from this same land.

During the eighteenth and nineteenth centuries, the highlands of western North Carolina witnessed virtually no social or economic progress. One of the chief reasons for the lack of change was topog-raphy. (Haywood County possesses more mountain peaks higher than 6000 feet above sea level than any other county east of the Mississippi River.) As the nation grew westward, sizeable settlements sprang up in areas that were more accessible outside of the mountains. Supplies had to be trucked in as far as the roads could go. Beyond that, crude trails provided the only means to carry in supplies on foot, by mule or on horseback. Some families had no road access to their property at all.

A couple of hundred years ago, plain-spoken, pragmatic pioneers in the Great Smoky Mountains had to rely on the land, themselves, and each other in order to survive. From the late 1700's until the early 1900's – when Cecil was a young child – mountaineers grew all their own food except for sugar and coffee, and they made all their own clothes. They fattened hogs on acorns to provide meat during the long winter months.

Until the second half of the twentieth century, both a solidly en-trenched culture and an aversion to outside influences kept social and technological progress at bay. While the area retained its rustic charm and culture, mountain residents had no contact with the outside world. Given their Dutch heritage, they were hardworking, willful, and self-reliant. But they also suspected anyone and anything that was alien to their culture. The absence of communication via telephones and radio added to their fear of strangers, even people from nearby areas.

Mountaineers had their own superstitions, home remedies, customs and mores. They believed in God and made their own "likker." In the 1920's, prohibition heightened their distrust of outsiders, since any approaching stranger might be a federal agent. The stock market crash of 1929 and the Great Depression had almost no impact in an area where life was already a perpetual struggle to survive. Since people grew their own food, they had no need to spend food stamps on meats and vegetables. Residents also lacked the modern conveniences taken for granted by outside civilization – running water, electricity, modern farm machinery, and indoor plumbing. Many of these amenities would not abound in the Smokies until as late as 1950.

Education for some families was merely a luxury, and if distance or seasonal work interfered, the children simply stayed at home. With limited access to school and little use for formal learning, young people had few chances to prepare for more lucrative jobs away from the mountains. Consequently, most of them grew up, married, and raised their families in the vicinity, perpetuating a cycle of abject poverty and seclusion from one generation to the next.

Yet the simplicity and isolation of mountain life, devoid of outside temptations, provided fertile ground for mission work. These unassuming folk upheld traditional virtues like hospitality, loyalty, fidelity, true friendship, personal responsibility and integrity. They were modest, humble, genuine people. Many of them had never attended a religious service, listened to a sermon, or heard the Bible read aloud. Clearly, they needed God's grace to give meaning and purpose to their lives, which were filled with little other than relentless work, hard times, illness, and death.

Into this appalling spiritual vacuum stepped a native daughter with strong faith, a fervent commitment to discipleship, and a singularity of purpose – Captain Cecil Brown. She would create a landmark ministry that would become a legend in the Great Smoky Mountains. Her extraordinary passion for the mountains, where she spent the vast majority of her life, would be exceeded only by a sacrificial love for its people.

A CRUSADER

Various churches had tried unsuccessfully to transcend the cultural obstacles to progress in western North Carolina. Finally, a most unlikely crusader appeared from within these very hollows. Cecil Brown took on what seemed an insurmountable task – to lift her people above the gloom of poverty and the despair of sin. Cecil wanted to put as many people as possible on the high road to heaven. By the time she joined the Salvation Army as a soldier, attended training college and received an appointment to the Mountain Mission, God had prepared her to be exactly what her people needed.

Daisy Cecil Brown was born on December 31, 1906 to Joseph and Maggie Brown in a two-room log house. She grew up on a farm in Hurricane Creek, N.C., a sparsely settled valley with steep sides and one winding dangerous road, if you could call it a "road." While it was possible to enter Hurricane Creek by foot or on horseback, the trail became treacherous when it rained or snowed. The uncertain terrain explains why no church bell had ever echoed through this valley, and only the occasional Methodist circuit rider had passed through.

Cecil enjoyed a happy childhood along with her three sisters and her three brothers. To accommodate the growing family, Joseph, who was a farmer and carpenter, built a six-room log house at Hurricane Creek. He kept the smokehouse full of choice meat, and his family always had plenty to eat. While snowed in for two or three months during the winter, they spent the time knitting stockings from their own sheep and preparing for the spring and summer months. Until the weather warmed up again, the family had virtually no contact with civilization.

In the Brown family, boys and girls worked both at home and in the fields. "My brothers can bake a pie as good as I can," Cecil said, "but I can use a rifle as accurately as they. Father used to keep his rifle on a peg over the door and the girls had equal access to it with the boys, and if the horses needed to be teamed up, either sisters or brothers could do the job." An unusually egalitarian upbringing helped to give Cecil the self-confidence she would need to succeed in a man's world.

A CIRCUIT RIDER

Cecil's tutor was a young woman who worked for Maggie in exchange for room and board and a monthly salary of $20 in cash. "I stayed in the seventh grade until I wore my books out," she explained. Seventh grade, which was as far as the teacher could take her students, focused on geography, history, spelling and arithmetic. Cecil repeated these subjects during three four-month spans, squeezing from them the last bit of information that she could.

As with most mountain youth, her childhood was filled with school, chores, play, and family life, with very little break from the everyday routine. Then, at the age of twelve, Cecil had an encounter that would change the course of her life. One day she left home and started out with her dog, walking five miles across the mountains to the country store. There she learned that a new preacher had arrived, and he had announced his plan to hold a series of revival meetings in Hurricane Creek. His idea met with much laughter, because the little community held a grand total of 20 people. Still, Cecil was intrigued.

Knowing well the maze of mountain trails, she decided to try and help the minister find his way. She took a shortcut to catch up with the small man who was struggling with his heavyset wife, two babies and a buggy full of their belongings. He looked worn out and at a loss when Cecil appeared, seemingly out of the blue.

"Can I help you?" she asked. The minister seemed grateful to let someone else ease his burden. So Cecil took the horse's bridle and led him down the shaky mountain path. When the buggy capsized and the preacher panicked, Cecil freed the trapped pastor's wife, she calmed the babies down, and she brought water in a cup made of leaves to bathe the family's scratches. Then the embattled group reached a place where a downed tree blocked their path – with no detour in sight – and the buggy became stuck in a thicket of branches.

A resourceful young Cecil quickly found the solution to the problem. "Take the wheels off and let the horse pull the chassis," she urged. Her suggestion worked, and eventually the weary party arrived safely in Hurricane Creek.

Meeting at the Schoolhouse

That night Cecil attended the evangelist's meeting in the schoolhouse. She later noted, "That man's preaching did something to my heart. I went to his meetings for two weeks. Then came a Saturday morning and the close of the revival series. The preacher invited us to come and kneel at the front. There were 15 people present and all of them responded to the invitation, but I was the very first. I didn't know what to pray except, 'Now I lay me down to sleep.' So I prayed that prayer. But I felt no different. Then I remembered a prayer I had sometimes heard my mother utter: 'Lord, forgive me.' I prayed it simply and sincerely."

God's Spirit touched Cecil's heart, and immediately she began to think about how to witness to others as well as meet their everyday needs. She felt seized by a determination to learn everything she could, beginning with an exhaustive study of the New Testament. On Sundays, she forfeited her leisure time in her cherished tree house to study, read, and practice teaching a Sunday School class. The seeds of service had taken root in fertile soil.

Identifying the mission sites

Chapter 3

The Move to Asheville

When Cecil reached the tender age of 16 years old, her mother permitted her to visit her older brother Fletcher in nearby Asheville. She arrived in the city resplendent in a brown pleated serge skirt and a matching velvet jacket with red buttons down the front. Her outfit had been ordered for eight dollars from Montgomery Ward. Sporting brown shoes and a matching hat, the young mountain girl braced for the big city. On her first day there, seeking to fulfill a vow she had made to God, she asked her brother to suggest a suitable church home.

"Church?" asked Fletcher. "The people will just laugh at you in church. The people here go to church to show off their finery. There isn't any church in Asheville with a speck of religion."

Meanwhile, Fletcher's wife, turning to more worldly concerns, thought that Cecil should get a job. She took Cecil downtown to a dime store that hired strong mountain girls who were willing to stand behind counters for long hours and little pay. The shy, insecure young girl prayed that no one would hire her and thus uncover her "ignorance." Despite her prayers, however, she was hired on the spot.

"All night," she said, "I prayed earnestly that they'd fire me quick, so the disgrace would be short. I was scared at the prospect and afraid to face people," she admitted, "but the Lord was working things out for me."

CHURCH HOME

The distance from Hurricane Creek to Asheville was only 55 miles, but to Cecil, who had never ventured outside of the mountains before,

Asheville seemed like another world. She had exchanged a quiet, simple life for the din of traffic and the modern wonders of electricity and indoor plumbing.

Fletcher turned out to be right about church — city worship did not feel like worship at all to a mountain native. In the mountains, people held services whenever and wherever they could find the time and place. The leader stood up without accompaniment and established the key and rhythm, with the congregation following joyfully along. In Asheville, worship was rigid and as regular as clockwork. Choirs routinely led music to the subdued notes of an organ amidst the hues of stained-glass windows. The two worship styles differed vastly, and Cecil longed for the familiarity of home.

Just before rush hour one Saturday evening at the store, she prepared to leave for her 30-minute supper break when a young man wearing a trim blue uniform came in to buy a pencil.

"I thought he was a mighty small policeman!" said Cecil. "Then I noticed the insignia on his cap … S.A., and asked someone what it meant. When I got home I asked Fletcher: 'What is The Salvation Army?'"

"Say," he replied, "I hadn't thought about that. You can go there to church tomorrow. They are the only people in town with any decent religion anyway!" Although Asheville was nowhere near a modern-day Sodom and Gomorrah, she now knew that there was at least one church she could attend where she just might feel comfortable in the city.

HER FIRST ARMY MEETING

So on a crisp Sunday morning in October 1924, Cecil Brown's fate was sealed as she entered an Army hall for the first time. Everything about the Army beckoned her – the smart uniforms, its spiritedness, and a simple atmosphere that made her feel welcome. Their hearty brand of worship reminded her of home. Even though she had never heard of the Salvation Army before, she immediately she knew it was where she belonged.

Recalling that first service 14 years later, she remarked, "I must say I didn't hear much of the sermon, for I sat behind two well-dressed Army lassies and their bonnets intrigued me. I spent the entire meeting trying to figure out how that headgear was made!"

After attending her first open-air meeting, Cecil returned with the group to the chapel. She went to all of the services, day and night, sitting in the back or standing off to the side. She was so enthralled with the Army that she even sat through their tedious committee and business meetings.

Her first Sunday marked the beginning of a revival series that continued for two weeks. Cecil continued to attend faithfully every time the doors opened, well into the following year. By spring, she was thoroughly indoctrinated with Salvation Army discipline and terminology.

THE DILEMMA

Oddly enough, at first no one urged her to join the corps. After six months as an "unofficial" recruit, someone finally asked her why she hadn't joined. Cecil replied that she would love to, and within a week the corps officer gave her a formal invitation along with the necessary documents to read and sign. It was a day that she had been secretly longing for. When her full-dress uniform and bonnet arrived COD, she paid with savings from her $10 a week salary at the dime store. On March 14, 1925, her divisional commander, Brigadier Arthur Hopkins, enrolled her as a soldier. She was 18 years old.

No sooner had Cecil settled in than she had to make a decision that would mark a turning point in her life. She was asked to work late one Thursday evening, but she wanted to attend an Army open-air meeting in the town square. When faced with the choice between a visceral call to preach and the mundane chore of preparing consumer goods to sell, she had no trouble making up her mind. Although the store manager had agreed to find a replacement, Cecil quickly received word that she had been fired.

Two days after she joined the other soldiers at the corner of Pack Square, she collected her last paycheck. With her cash capital depleted from the purchase of her new uniform, she had no income or savings left to live on. Her corps officer, Captain Dorothy Guice, a spiritual woman with a magnetic personality, would have gladly helped Cecil, had she only asked. But Cecil did not think about seeking the captain's help to find a new position. As a stoic mountain girl, she had no experience in asking for favors graciously. Her ancestors had made their own way unaided against the worst that nature and fortune could present. After two weeks of fruitlessly searching for another job, she decided to return home. It was a heartbreaking decision, because her life was now entirely wrapped up in her Army ministry.

Cecil's belief that her family did not need her back on the farm in Hurricane Creek only worsened her melancholy mood. Her future, she had concluded, lay in building the kingdom of God. Nonetheless, she planned to return to Waynesville by train and ride back into the Smokies on a logging truck. At Fletcher's suggestion, however, she decided to stay for four more weekly meetings and one last open-air service. She had no way of knowing that God had other plans in store for her.

A SOLUTION

That Sunday, a concerned Captain Guice was trying to sort out a troublesome predicament of her own. Her lieutenant had been transferred to another appointment, and she needed a new assistant. After the Sunday night meeting, Cecil finally unburdened her dilemma and she began to tell her captain goodbye.

Captain Guice was overjoyed. "I would have asked you weeks ago to come and live with me and help in the work, but I was unwilling to suggest that you quit your job," she replied.

The next morning, a relieved Cecil moved in with the captain and began her work as the unofficial assistant of the Asheville corps. Later, in 1929, at the age of 22, she entered the training college in Atlanta. She received her commission as a Salvation Army officer with brief appointments to the training college staff and as a corps officer in Statesville (1931), Goldsboro and Salisbury (1933). She also started the Army's work in Reidsville. During the next seven years, God's will for her specific life calling would began to fall into place.

Cecil (at left) with her cadet colleagues

Chapter 4

Starting Out at Shelton Laurel

Shelton Laurel is not a town. It is not even a dot on the map. There is no post office there. Not even a general store.

It actually resembles more of a neighborhood. If we had to point to a specific location for Shelton Laurel, it could be a one-room schoolhouse. From that schoolhouse, however, there is not even a home in sight.

The road leading from the schoolhouse winds back down the mountain through laurel and rhododendron thickets. When Cecil Brown decided to launch the Mountain Mission from Shelton Laurel, she found about 23 families living there, a total of 95 people.

Shelton Laurel, though an ideal springboard for organized religion, had been neglected by the established church for at least eight years. A Methodist circuit rider used to preach and offer limited pastoral care there once a month, but residents could not meet the preacher's modest $25 salary. One church held a part-time Sunday School about five miles away on another mountain, and occasionally someone from Shelton Laurel would attend. However, most of the children born after the circuit rider stopped coming had never worshipped in a church, never heard of Sunday School or even a gospel hymn. If a family owned a Bible at all, they often left it on a shelf to gather dust.

This was a field ready for harvest. Mothers yearned for someone to teach the Word of God to their children, and fathers openly hungered for a place where they could bring their families to worship. These spiritually starved people welcomed Cecil as a beacon of hope to their isolated community. They assured her that if she started a Sunday School and a monthly church service, they would somehow find $25 to pay her salary. She epitomized manna from heaven to folks who felt deserted and yearned for a relationship with God. Cecil made a preliminary visit to each of the 23 homes. During each one she announced to the family that a Sunday School would be conducted that next week in the schoolhouse.

The Sheep's Bell

When that red-letter Sunday arrived in late February, Cecil was still living in Waynesville. She had to get up at six a.m. that morning to reach Shelton Laurel by 10 a.m. She drove as far as her rubber tires would allow in the wintry weather, then she hiked the remaining four miles through mud and snow. Fifty-four people, many who had never attended church before, came to greet her. By noon, four more people came in out of the snow, bringing the total attendance to 58.

Cecil organized four classes, and each class elected a teacher. A high school graduate, aided by a young schoolteacher, agreed to be the Sunday School superintendent. During the first church service, 14 people responded to the altar call following the sermon. Cecil felt convinced that the receptiveness in Shelton Laurel mirrored a widespread openness to spirituality throughout the mountains.

An urgent need for Sunday school teachers reminded her of a practical tool that had been used on her family's farm in Hurricane Creek. Her father had tied a bell around a sheep's neck so that the rest of the aimless flock would follow his lead. Cecil decided to use this same technique to appoint a spiritual leader from within the local community. Afterwards, the reluctant nominee came to her and announced, "You've made a big mistake, Miss Cecil. I can't be the leader of the Sunday school. All the people here know what kind of man I am."

"Then why don't you start being different?" Cecil retorted. She went on to explain how God could change him, and that is exactly what happened.

Home League

In addition to a deep spiritual void, Captain Brown encountered pressing temporal needs among the people as well. She successfully appealed to other corps for donations of clothes, and the women formed a Home League group to sort and distribute them to needy children. For years to come, thousands of boxed garments from all over the South would go to poor children who attended Sunday School in the mountains.

Cecil also put donations of cloth to good use. "I find the women here are making beautiful patchwork quilts, and we could do many things if we had something to work with," she wrote to headquarters.

The Asheville *Citizen* picked up the story, which prompted a letter from a destitute woman who lived on a nearby mountain. "I understand you are helping the mountain people," she wrote. "I am a mountain woman and the mother of 10 children. My eldest son is working his way through high school and I have five children going to school without shoes and badly in need of clothes." Cecil immediately established a rapport with this family.

During that first spring rain and snow made travel difficult. But the bad weather did not deter people, and it did little to slow Cecil down.

"I'm getting along fine with my work," she wrote in one report to her divisional commander, "but it seems to rain every Sunday, and this means a number of miles walking through the mud. I'm getting to be quite a hiker. The most I have walked in one day so far is 23 miles."

By Easter, the Shelton Laurel Mission was firmly in place. On Easter Sunday the children celebrated with an egg hunt. Families who had been unchurched for years voiced their desire for a two-week revival series between the winter snows and spring planting. The revival would be a watershed event for the mountain mission!

"LADY PREACHER"

Although the people initially requested two weeks of revival meetings, Cecil decided to limit the campaign to one week. In three short months, she had organized a faithful congregation, a weekly Sunday School with local leadership, and regular worship services. Not everything, however, had run as smoothly. The locals appreciated her visits, the Sunday School, and even her bold, authoritative personality, but consensus stopped short on the subject of a female preacher. As in the outside world, women had the freedom to pursue traditionally female occupations such as nursing, social work, health, homemaking and gardening to feed the family. Preaching, however, was an occupation that did not cross gender lines for them. "No woman could holler and shout loud enough to make a good preacher anyhow," one mountain man said.

The people pondered this lively topic of conversation from the lumber mill to as far down the mountain as the filling station. A rousing debate peaked at the same time that Cecil Brown personally carried news of the upcoming revival into every single home. Male employees at the lumber mill held heated discussions about "that woman preacher" who was scheduled as the featured speaker.

The long-awaited revival debuted before a capacity crowd in the small schoolhouse. It seated about 60 people comfortably, but that night 150 people crowded into the chapel to hear Cecil preach. Those who lived far away had to leave early to get there on time. Many of them walked several miles with lanterns to illuminate the dark mountain trails on the way home.

The news of the revivals spread quickly by word of mouth. The large assembly drew both curiosity-seekers and people who were eager to hear the Word of God. One man crossed the mountains from a distant community when he heard that Shelton Laurel was hosting a female preacher. He did not return home until four a.m. the next morning.

All of Shelton Laurel's preachers had been short-lived. There was a rumor that the rough part of the community would not allow someone to preach more than three nights in a row. So, on the third night of the revival when Cecil spotted a tall, unidentified man circling the schoolhouse, she grew understandably anxious. The man turned out to be the deputy sheriff, who had been enlisted to ensure Cecil's safety and to prevent the disruption of her services. "The first man that comes here with even the smell of whiskey on his breath, off he goes to jail," he promised.

The first convert was Xavier Lamb, a former church member who had abandoned his faith eight years before. The congregation laughed when he gave his testimony, but he became the Sunday School superintendent of Paint Rock Union Church, and he oversaw more than 100 children. Another man, who lay awake nights because of the noise, decided to attend a meeting out of sheer exasperation. Not only was he saved but Cecil went home with him to Bonnie Hill where his wife also committed her life to Christ. He became the corps sergeant major, and even after moving away, he continued to walk 14 miles every Sunday to lead the meetings there.

THE DOUBTING COOK

Five people came forward to yield their will to Christ, and many others approached the altar because they felt profoundly moved. By the end of the week, it became clear that the revival should be extended into a second week. Meanwhile, opponents of women preachers came to see what was happening, including the cook at the lumber mill. The cook had no use for religion in general, disliked women preachers in particular, and had earned a reputation for using choice profanity.

As soon as he entered the chapel, Cecil knew he was a stranger. But she was unaware of his loose tongue and the emptiness in his soul. He listened intently to Cecil's sermon, and then the Holy Spirit gently touched his heart. After Captain Brown gave the invitation, the cook went forward and knelt publicly at the altar. He testified for the rest of his life about the night he became "a new creature in Christ Jesus."

By the next morning the news of the cook's conversion had spread all over the lumber camp. In the kitchen, others curiously observed him bending over his pots on the stove to prepare breakfast. Then came the defining moment in his newfound faith, when an incident occurred that usually would have unleashed a stream of profanity. The pot of rice burned! Amazingly, he had no problem curbing his temper in front of this group of astonished onlookers. Even more remarkably, he not only stopped cursing but joined Cecil Brown as a trusted dispenser of good will.

SOWING AND REAPING

Successful inroads at Shelton Laurel paved the way for progress elsewhere in the Mountain Mission. By the end of the second week of meetings, ten more men and women had dedicated their lives to Christ. Seventy-five people requested prayer, and many of them later enrolled as soldiers. An unsolicited offering at the close of the second week of meetings affirmed the compelling power of the gospel message. The same community that eight years earlier could not find $25 to pay the Methodist circuit preacher now experienced a burst of generosity.

Cecil wrote to Major Gilks: "At the close of the meeting they took up a collection which amounted to $9.21 in cash and an order to a gas station for 18 gallons of gas. Some of the women brought an offering of canned goods. I was almost surprised beyond words for I had not said a word about money up to this time. It came as a pleasant surprise."

With Shelton Laurel running smoothly, Cecil turned her attention to other potential missions. In a report to divisional headquarters, she wrote: "Last Sunday night, I conducted a meeting in the Fines Creek

Methodist Church, and there were more than 200 people present in the church, not counting those on the outside looking through the windows and doors. I certainly do not lack for inspiration!"

WAYNE AND FANNY

Octogenarian Wayne Moore is the current lay leader of the Shelton Laurel Corps. Wayne, a corps sergeant major for more than 45 years, gave a first-hand account of his indirect conversion to Christianity as a result of Cecil's ministry. He was, by his own testimony, still "a wild young man sowing his oats," and he admitted a genuine awe for Cecil. He credits her with having "planted the seeds of faith in (his) heart." After Brigadier James Henry succeeded Major Brown, Wayne committed his life to God.

"I think she was successful in doing what she did here in the mountains because she was a mountain girl," he said. "She knew people. She knew how to get to them. She knew how to talk to them.

"Even those who were not saved respected what she did for all of us. You might even say we had a healthy fear of her. For instance, there was the time long before I was saved, when a bunch of us were going fishing at Cold Springs. We got a quarter-ton truck, and there were about eight or ten people riding with us. I was driving the truck – it belonged to my father-in-law.

"I didn't know that some of the people on board had brought home-made liquor with them. Now I drank a little back then, but I didn't know until we had left to go fishing that there was some moonshine in that truck.

"We were driving down the road not too far from one of Cecil Brown's churches, and there was this turn in the road. It was a sharp turn. I got a little too far over, and she came around the bend and had to run off the road and into the water ditch to avoid hitting us.

"She got out of her jeep and said she believed she'd call the law on us. Now, remember, I didn't know it at that moment, but two of the guys with me had, I think it was, two half-gallon jars of white liquor on them.

"No one said anything, but we were all nervous about her maybe calling the law – especially those two boys who knew that they had the liquor with them. Well, anyway, she changed her mind, and told us to behave ourselves. She told us to be more careful and not to get into any more trouble."

"Cecil had a way of convincing people to attend church, especially for special things like the Singing Convention," Wayne added.

Fanny Rathbone, another Salvationist from Cecil's generation, still attends the Shelton Laurel Corps. She is in her nineties now. Her family played a prominent role in the history of the Mountain Mission, and she has attended every Singing Convention since it started when she was 16 years old.

"I used to see Major Brown almost every day," Fanny said. "She would come to get me and I would help her with whatever she had to do in her ministry. She certainly did a lot for my family and me. She always came by to take me to church. Otherwise, I couldn't have gone. I had no other way to go to church."

Brigadier James Henry held a special place in his heart for Shelton Laurel. His retirement home, up until the time of his Promotion to Glory in 2004, was just a few steps from the site of the present corps building. The building had to be moved during his administration.

"The structure that housed the Shelton Laurel Corps is historic. Strangely enough, the living room of the present officers' quarters was the church," said the Brigadier. "General Frederick Coutts preached in that one little room, and so did General Clarence Wiseman and General Albert Orsborn!"

When the Army decided to move the building, just around the bend of the mountain, it was still a one-room church house/schoolhouse combination. "We put that tiny structure on a mule shed, and pulled it five miles around the mountain here, and propped it up on rocks. That's where it is today," he said.

The personal touch

Chapter 5

Turning Toward Home

For the next mission opening, Cecil Brown turned her eyes toward home. In Hurricane Creek, where she grew up, the need remained as great as when she was a little girl. Her ancestral home was still there.

Excitement quickly spread when the people of Hurricane Creek learned that they would soon reap the benefits of the same awe-inspiring work being done at Shelton Laurel. The plan for launching and nurturing the mountain missions now had a definite shape.

Hurricane Creek had a small schoolhouse with one room where children received a basic education just four months out of the year. The schoolhouse doubled as an educational, social and cultural center for about 75 families living in a seven-mile radius. Many people remembered back when "Miss Cecil" was a young student in that same one-room structure. Now, she was back again, wearing a blue uniform, and announcing from cabin to cabin the start of a regular Sunday School.

When Sunday arrived, Cecil stood in the same room where she had almost worn out her seventh-grade books from so much studying. Only this time she held her open Bible and a Sunday School lesson that she was ready to teach. She stood in the same spot, behind the same desk, as her own teachers had stood years before. Contrary to the adage of noted Asheville author Thomas Wolfe, *she had gone home again.*

Despite all the confidence Cecil exuded throughout her life, her diary continued to reflect her personal insecurities. In one entry, she critiqued her sermon to the congregation at Hurricane Creek. "I spoke on the 'Parable of the Sower.' We had a good attendance, but I failed in my sermon. Better next time," she wrote.

Cecil's greatest limitation was that she could visit only two locations each Sunday. Her mornings were spent at Shelton Laurel and her afternoons at Hurricane Creek, with a meeting and Sunday School at each mission. What she did in her first opening was, of necessity, repeated in her second one.

"As the crow flies," the mileage between missions was not huge, but when winter rains and snows bogged down the trails, the 15-mile distance seemed like 150.

According to Brigadier Dorothy Langston, snow in the mountains sometimes got so deep that Cecil and her aides had to tunnel their way to the outhouse. Once she was snowed in so badly that her cabin was completely covered and she had to dig out through the windows just to let air inside.

When Major Gilks wrote to Cecil with the suggestion, "Buy a horse!" – Cecil, who was just as practical, readily agreed. "You had a good idea to get a horse to ride all over the mountains. I have been praying that I could get one, but there are so few up here that the people who own one will not think of selling it for less than $125. However, it would aid me much in my travels and maybe a little later if I can get one."

Shortly after that letter, she did buy a horse named "Dolly," that helped her to negotiate muddy roads and treacherous mountain ledges. Years later, Doris Morgan's famous painting of her, sitting fully-uniformed astride her horse, would be indelibly engraved in the hearts and minds of Smoky Mountain residents. Riding horseback would become her favorite mode of transportation.

The famous passage from Isaiah 52:7, that was used as a caption with the painting, offers a fitting tribute to Cecil. "*How beautiful upon the mountains are the feet of the messenger who announces peace, who brings good news, who announces salvation, who says to Zion, 'Your God reigns.'*" This oft-quoted scripture celebrates the 600-mile journey of an emissary running 600 miles from Babylon to Jerusalem to announce that the Jewish exiles had been freed to return home. Now, roughly 2,600 years later, Cecil Brown was bringing the gospel message of hope and salvation to people in western North Carolina.

It had been only three short months since she had arrived in Waynesville, full of energy, spirit, and acumen. As she rode Dolly along the rugged mountain trails, she had plenty of time to survey the fruit of her labors. One of her reports, dated toward the end of April, informed Major Gilks optimistically: "Yesterday was a pretty day and we had a fine time up here in the mountains. In the morning, I went to Shelton Laurel. We had 119 folks in Sunday School. After the morning service, I went to my second center at Hurricane Creek where we had 108 in attendance. I conducted Sunday School and service there and we had a fine spirit in both meetings. The roads were dry and I did not have to walk to either place. This was a great help."

Ironically, gender and limited education would become two of Cecil's greatest assets over time. Some people attended her meetings out of curiosity, others in appreciation for her message and mission. Most people believed that she had honorable intentions and a sincere desire to help them, and her indigenous ties to the area helped to win the respect of lifelong mountaineers.

People crowded into the tiny Hurricane Creek schoolhouse just as they had done in Shelton Laurel. Mothers sent their children to Sunday School, and congregations revived old hymns, to the great delight of the aging parishioners. Many children were learning the compelling story of Jesus for the first time in their lives.

The real test for Cecil and the Smoky Mountain Mission came when evil challenged the power of the gospel. Without the positive influence of a church, people had fallen prey to the sinful ways of life. Cecil's challenge was to bring a message that could permanently transform their lives.

Soon after Sunday meetings began, the people of Hurricane Creek requested a series of revivals. The time seemed ripe, and so dates were set for early the next spring. Announcements passed quickly from neighbor to neighbor. From adjoining valleys, other families heard the news and they too wanted to join in the meetings.

This time, however, Cecil enlisted an elderly Moravian minister, a preacher who immediately established rapport with the people. She led spirited singing that complemented his fiery sermons. Together they drew capacity crowds every night.

Including visitors from "outside the mountains," crowds often totaled 200 - 300 people. Fewer than half that number were able to pack the schoolhouse – the remainder of the crowd had to watch through the windows or stand in the doorway. But the people seemed to enjoy the good fellowship and the gospel singing as much as they did the sermons. Some families made a habit of arriving an hour or two early to enjoy the preliminary singing before the actual service began.

The singing in those missions was unlike most worship in the city. Mountain worship was hearty and nearly fever-pitched, while city worship was usually led by choirs and the singing came from cushioned pews. It often sounded like humming – just above a whisper. In the city, churches chose mostly "classical" hymns, while in the mountains people sang songs that had been passed down from memory.

In the mountains families observed the traditional Amish custom of separating men and women in the chapel. Younger children sat with their mothers, although older boys were allowed to sit with the men. The entire meeting evoked a jubilant noise unto the Lord, a celebration that was an anomaly in most sophisticated urban areas. People worshipped, went forward to pray and usually left transformed. Three hundred people attended the first Sunday afternoon revival in Hurricane Creek. Many of them brought a meal to eat, arriving early enough to make sure they got a seat. The overflow crowd remained outside within earshot.

This lively series of meetings led to the vital decision to build a church there. No building campaign had to take place because a landowner promptly donated a plot of ground for the site. The nearest sawmill offered to donate the material for flooring and then agreed to sell the rest of the lumber at wholesale price. The poorer folk donated their labor. Only the foreman and a stonemason received compensation for their work.

Before that summer ended, Cecil also envisioned a headquarters for her work in a suitable building in or near Hurricane Creek, then she briefly turned away from this task to visit other communities in need.

Cecil felt at home on horseback.

Chapter 6

Cecil's Extended Family

Blanche Lowe lived with Cecil and other young female lieutenants in the Mountain Mission headquarters at Maple Springs. Blanche, a native of the mountains, was practically raised by Cecil.

"Our little community center at Maple Springs was like one big family," she recalled. "We each had chores. We had a well that we had to pump our water from in order to have water inside the house. We had no mechanical pump – *we* were the pumps!" she laughed.

"We had our work schedule posted on a bulletin board for a week at a time. We each knew what our chores were. For instance, I would pump water for about 15 minutes, then go feed the chickens, collect their eggs, and milk the cows. We had pigs at one time and we had to take care of them!" Cecil always assigned Blanche to milk the cows because she was the only person who knew how!

"At a small store we established called the Trading Post," Blanche said, "the women displayed and sold towels and rugs that they had woven."

Cecil spoke candidly about her grueling routine while working at Maple Springs. "Life was difficult. I was often gone for long periods from my barn headquarters, and sometimes went for days without even looking into a mirror."

In one letter she wrote, "It has been snowing out at the citadel for over a week. I spent my first night out there last Saturday and on Sunday morning there was a small blanket of snow on my bed that had come in through the cracks. Outside, the snow was eight inches deep."

THELMA HALL

Thelma Hall also came to Maple Springs to live and work with Cecil. Thelma's father worked for the lumber mill that figured so prominently in the success of the Mountain Mission. She is the only person from there who ever became a Salvation Army officer.

"Cecil Brown had the Maple Springs Citadel in operation by the time I met her in 1938," Thelma said. "Her family had built the structure, as well as the springhouse and other buildings surrounding the corps. We were never idle for one minute. We kept on the go all the time. She got up in the morning with something to do and when we weren't going to school she kept us busy."

"Cecil provided a home and an education for the children who came from very remote areas. Children lived with her there because their families lived too far from the nearest place where the school buses could come," Blanche said. "That was the beginning of what we called the Children's Home, although it wasn't a children's home in the way that people today would think of one. Aside from offering a tremendous ministry, it allowed Cecil to train the girls to be potential leaders in the Mountain Mission. She was always searching for that one person who could take her place after she retired."

Cecil recognized leadership potential in Thelma Hall. "The influence Cecil had on my life was wonderful," Thelma recalled. "She used to say, 'Thelma, I think you would do well to come back to the mountains and run things here after I'm gone.' But I didn't feel called to go back to the mountains, and I felt that God was leading me in another direction."

"I visited the site about two years ago," Thelma said solemnly. "Today a family lives in the building that used to house the Maple Springs Corps. There is no more citadel. There is no more Salvation Army there. The only thing left is the old cemetery. My husband and I went into that cemetery – it is all fenced in and the area is still beautiful, although it has changed so much over the years, and so many things that I remember there are now gone."

Before the citadel was built, Rich Mountain, located about eight miles from Maple Springs, had a seventy-five year old log cabin meeting house. A Sunday School opened there, and a graduate from the Moody Bible Institute volunteered to teach. Two thousand feet of lumber was donated, and a mountain woman made the first donation of a dollar, which Cecil promptly put into an old teapot for safekeeping.

MILDRED FOLEY

The search for new assistants and a possible replacement for Cecil extended to other parts of the Tar Heel state. Mildred Foley, who lived in a small North Carolina community and attended Youth Councils, was tapped as a potential successor. Mildred worked with Cecil for a short time before entering the Army's training college, a practice not uncommon to Captain Brown. She had spent more than three years working with Cecil before she left.

"When she saw me at Youth Councils, she said to me, 'What are you doing now? Have you graduated from high school?' I told her that I hadn't and that I had one more year – and then I planned to go to the training college," Mildred said.

"She said, 'Why don't you come work for me? You can go to school up here and work for me, and then I'll send you to training.'

"I told her I didn't think I could do that. I really didn't think about it any more – that is, until the Sunday morning of the Youth Councils. Cecil came to me and said, 'Did you think any more about what I asked you?'"

Mildred again deferred her answer.

"Later, it was right after lunch and Daddy was there," Mildred went on, "so I told him that Cecil Brown was here and that she asked me to go to work for her and go to school in the mountains. I was so sure he'd say, 'Oh no, you're not going anywhere!'

"But he didn't. Instead he asked me, 'What do you want to do? Have you prayed about it?'

"I really prayed about it, and I really didn't want to go, but I finally said to the Lord, 'Well, I'll give it a shot if You want me to go.'"

Mildred later discovered that her friends had predicted she would not last more than a week working with Cecil Brown.

DEAN SELF

Still another possible protégé under consideration was a young woman named Dean Self.

"Major Brown begged my Daddy – to allow me to go and work with her as one of her assistants," Dean said. "Of course, my Daddy said, 'No.' He wanted to keep our family together. But I often wonder what my life would have been like if I had worked alongside her."

Dean's move to Bonnie Hill, N.C., as a toddler had coincided with Cecil's arrival to open a corps there. To Dean, this dynamic Salvation Army officer, who later enrolled her as a junior solder, appeared larger than life. Dean graduated from the Army's training college in 1965 and served as a Salvation Army officer for many years. She has such a deep love and abiding respect for Cecil that she keeps a copy of Cecil's death certificate in a scrapbook along with other cherished photos and mementos.

(Lorraine) Jean Frese

Major Jean Frese probably came closest to being Cecil's heir-apparent. Jean and Cecil shared a special bond, and Jean served many years in the Mountain Mission long after her mentor was promoted to Glory. She earned her officer's commission through the Salvation Army's auxiliary captaincy program, and she enjoyed two tours of duty in the Mountain Mission.

Her first appointment with Cecil Brown and a series of her successors lasted about 17 years, and her second one extended from 1976 until the mid-1980s. Now retired, she lives on the grounds of the present-day Shelton Laurel Corps, and she hopes to erect a memorial to Cecil at the Mountain Mission. Major Brown had a lasting impact on Jean's life and she prepared her to be an Army officer.

Jean vividly recalled the first time she met Cecil Brown while on a trip with friends. She had sat in the back seat of the late-model car, absorbing the grandeur around her, as the dusty road led up the steep mountain to Maple Springs, N.C., to Cecil's headquarters. Occasionally she would yawn to clear her ears as the car climbed higher and higher.

She had looked forward to this part of her vacation more than any other item on her itinerary. To a young city girl from Pittsburgh, this leg of the journey seemed uncomfortable and even scary, but it was exciting and exhilarating, too. The road was so bumpy and narrow that if two cars met from opposite directions, one had to pull over to let the other one by. Unofficially, the rule was that the vehicle traveling downhill always had the right of way. Sometimes a wall of rock on one side and a cliff on the other side meant there was no space to pull over. This usually meant the car coming up had to back down to the next place where the car coming down could pass.

Climbing out of the car, Jean instantly grew enchanted with the breathtaking beauty of the Great Smoky Mountains. Before her, with an extended hand of welcome, stood the lean, gaunt major with eyes that flickered. Cecil was already a legend by this time.

Over the next few days, Major Brown gave her guests a tour of the mission centers. By the end of the trip, Cecil recognized a potential assistant in Jean and asked her if she would consider returning to help with the mission work. At first Jean declined, but three years later she accepted the invitation.

Jean's given name was Lorraine, but because Cecil had another assistant with the same first name, she asked Lorraine if she had another name. The only other name Lorraine could think of was that of her mother, Jean. So from that moment on Lorraine Frese changed her name to Jean Frese – even in her official record at territorial headquarters. But Cecil's single-mindedness did not seem to bother Jean in the slightest – she respected and admired it.

"What was wonderful about Major Brown is that if you were trying to do what she told you to do, she would be behind you all the way," Jean said.

"She once said to me, 'Do you know how to make cornbread?'"

"I said, 'No – and I don't even know how to build a fire in this stove.'"

"She smiled and said, 'I'll do it for you and I'll show you how.' She was right there with you. She always wanted to help you to learn how to do things. One day she told me to go to the field and hoe weeds out of the garden, but I didn't know how to handle a hoe. I saw the way the others were hoeing and I said, 'All right, I think I can do this.'

"I took two strikes of that hoe, and then Cecil said, 'Go back to the house!'

"I was tearing up all the plants and leaving the weeds! That's the type of a person Cecil was. If you tried your best to do what she told you to do, she was right behind you to help you, but she never expected you to do what you couldn't – or didn't do well."

"She was all business," Jean continued. "When I first came, she told me to forget everything I had ever learned about driving. She was going to teach me how to drive in the mountains. Jeeps were not like cars."

GLENNA WEST

Major Glenna West also numbers among Cecil's beloved assistants. Glenna served as a Salvation Army officer for more than 42 years until she retired in 1994. She now lives in Asheville, almost within the shadow of the very mountains she loved as a child. All of her promotions in rank came during the several appointments that she served in the Mountain Mission.

"When you stop to think about it, Cecil Brown was a very progressive thinker. She did a lot of the things that we are doing today," Glenna said. "She was a good listener who was willing to accept suggestions from other people."

"She wanted to get people saved before they were enrolled as soldiers and put on that uniform. She wanted them trained for leadership. She was carrying out back then what we are emphasizing today: saving souls, growing saints and serving suffering humanity."

Maple Springs under a mantle of snow

Chapter 7

The Backwoods of Big Bend

The notorious hamlet of Big Bend easily ranked as the most colorful and dangerous of the dozen or so mission centers that Cecil Brown operated.

Big Bend, which was home to 44 adults and 31 children, was literally a big bend in the Pigeon River. To Cecil and her lieutenants, this Old West style setting resembled more of a Hollywood movie set than an actual place where real people lived. But there was nothing romantic about a feuding center where many men had been shot and killed, then buried, without the law being able to adjudicate. Big Bend was an anachronism. To make matters worse, a nine-mile footpath severed this surreal bastion of hostility from the outside world.

Cecil found unbelievable poverty and suffering there. The people couldn't afford to burn oil, so the only light most homes had came from burning ubiquitous pine knots. Without clocks to wake them up on time, children typically arrived at school a couple of hours late. Only two homes owned bed linen, and most people had only one outfit of clothing.

In Big Bend, the only jobs included menial labor at the lumber mill. Residents lived as they had for generations, eating what they grew, and drinking their homemade liquor, which only increased their problems. The one thing they had in abundance – besides pine knots – was moonshine. Stills were hidden all over the area. Making moonshine involved a community effort, and the people enjoyed drinking what they made. An outsider might say, "Well, that's all they had," which, up to a point, is probably true, but it didn't make their choice to consume it any easier on the community.

A fear of being discovered by revenuers intensified the prevailing distrust of outsiders. Not even a woman who hailed from the mountains could be trusted if there was the slightest chance that she would turn someone in for bootlegging.

Nonetheless, Cecil entered this cesspool of ignorance and want about 30 miles from the county seat of Waynesville with the same determination she showed in every other challenging situation.

The danger was not in going in – it was in coming out. Popular mountain lore told of people who had ventured there and were never seen again. It was a dangerous place, and people from the surrounding mountains usually shunned it. Moonshine and poverty were all they knew. Big Bend was literally another world.

One can only imagine that Cecil must have had at least a lump in her throat as she approached the tiny village. She wore her smart blue uniform, and probably relied on her reputation to carry the day. Fortunately, it did.

Every home received a visit from the "lady preacher." The people received her graciously and cordially. Cecil later commented to a relative that she didn't see any of the stills – they were that well hidden.

She read the Bible in every home and prayed for each family. She even encouraged each member of the family to kneel with her in prayer!

The poverty and ignorance was so appalling that Cecil would talk about it for the rest of her life. Nevertheless, the hospitality extended by some of the families left a lasting impression on her as well. One family, sensing the importance of her visit, told her that they had wanted to clean up – but they had no soap. The fact that they had no water system, no lamps, no linens of any kind, and no real furniture was somewhat understandable. But no soap?

The captain invited everyone, young and old, to attend her first meeting the following night. She noticed that all of the girls had long, tangled hair hanging down their backs. Approaching the problem of personal hygiene from the easiest and most diplomatic angle, Cecil asked one of the girls, "Anna, have you combed your hair today?"

"No, ma'am," Anna replied politely. "None of us ever combs our head, 'cause we ain't none of us got no combs!"

Cecil then gave Anna her own comb, and she resolved that more combs and other hygienic products must be provided for these children. Through Major Gilks, she again appealed to the Southern Territory, and generous donations came pouring in, just as they had through her clothing appeal.

By the time the first official meeting was held, a sudden rain had swollen the river and the water level rose up to the bend. Even though families living on one side of the mountain had to cross the river to reach the schoolhouse, high water did not prevent them from attending what, for many, was the first worship service of their lives.

"They have no way to cross the river when it rains except to swim and wade, but that is the way they came to attend our meetings, wading and swimming," Cecil said.

Captain Brown faithfully prepared both her heart and her mind for that first important meeting. It would lay the basis for any extended work to be done at Big Bend. She was, she later admitted, a little anxious. "I certainly had to do some praying and trusting to God for a message for them. They wanted the Bread of Life in a language they could understand. Only the help of God enabled me to tell the salvation story as it should be told."

She faced the congregation. For a moment or two, she doubted that the sermon she had prepared would be appropriate. She thought her material was all wrong. She discarded her notes, shifted gears, and began to tell them the story of Jesus – His birth, His life, His death and His resurrection. She told the people, who were sitting in spellbound silence, about this Man who was also God – who He was and what He came to do for them.

"It was just like explaining the whole story to a little child," she said later. "In fact, the children seemed to understand it much better than the adults did."

At the close of the meeting, a mother of six children thanked Cecil in her own humble way for coming. She explained that this was only the second time she had ever been in a religious meeting place. The first time was 26 years earlier when she had gone to a church to be married.

An elderly woman echoed her joy that a religious meeting had been conducted at Big Bend with a promise of many more to follow. She was old enough to remember one other long ago service. Ever since that day, she had prayed that God would spare her to hear another sermon and more prayer. She told Cecil that she had never traveled to Waynesville. In fact, she had never even been out of Big Bend!

Cecil had expected to do missionary work in the mountains, but the task of bringing Christian social graces to this district sometimes overwhelmed her. A year earlier, the county had started a school at Big Bend in a leaky 20-foot by 30-foot shack without any windows. The teacher who lived and worked at the schoolhouse owned the only radio in the area. With the nearest postal service 10 miles away at Mount Sterling, mail had to be called for by the owner and brought in by horseback. There was no delivery of newspapers or magazines. No doctors could be found in the vicinity.

From Mount Sterling, N.C., Captain Brown wrote in 1938, "In this Big Bend section, it is difficult to get a letter. My little song sheets are wearing out. I only have twelve and I need at least a hundred. I wish I could have more."

A SILENT ESCORT

Despite all the hazards surrounding Big Ben, no one ever harmed Cecil, but she must have felt threatened at least once. Hoping to hitch a ride back 25 miles to her main headquarters, she had started the nine-mile walk over the mountains to the main roads, when a young man appeared, took hold of her bag, and announced his intention to accompany her through the woods. Cecil knew that he had been acquitted of killing three men by reason of self-defense, so she decided not to argue with him. Following the mountain custom, he led the way, and she walked behind respectfully. He spoke to her just three times in response to questions she asked. When they reached the main road, he returned her bag, shook hands with her, and expressed thanks for her ministry. He promised that he would always guarantee her safety in Big Bend, and he urged her not to feel afraid.

Cecil had a single model to follow for her work at Big Bend, the same plan that she had used in Shelton Laurel and Hurricane Creek. She would see what a Sunday School and a monthly meeting would produce. She felt not only needed by the people of Big Bend – she felt wanted.

MOONSHINE

The closest thing to a misunderstanding Cecil had while working in Big Bend arose from a remark she made to a Charlotte newspaper reporter who asked her about trouble arising there from moonshine whiskey. Very tactfully, Cecil answered, "That is something we don't talk about."

Realizing that Cecil had cleverly stonewalled him, the reporter seized on her comment, and news of his story returned to the mountains and circled back to Big Bend. Even though making moonshine was illegal, the people viewed it as a personal matter that should not be mentioned outside of their area. Cecil wisely realized that her ministry would be threatened if the residents thought she was invading their privacy and interfering with their right to produce whiskey. So, with every visit to Big Bend, whatever she saw, she never reported. She won the trust of the people by remaining silent about their personal activities.

Cecil worried a lot about that newspaper article. The matter subsided with no apparent revenuer raids on the horizon. She then developed her own method of dealing with the liquor problem. Rather than advocating temperance or prohibition, she decided that the only cure was the grace of God in the life of each individual. If she could get people saved, she reasoned, sinful ills would vanish automatically. Salvation would succeed where prohibition and other types of control had failed.

Appreciation for her work at Big Bend grew steadily. She felt proud of her missions there, and at Shelton Laurel and Hurricane Creek. Following the usual procedure, she held a series of revival meetings at Big Bend, but this time the results proved disappointing.

THE GOSPEL IN ACTION

After the soul-stirring responses at Shelton Laurel and Hurricane Creek, Cecil expected the same end results at Big Bend, but only two converts came forth as a visible sign of that campaign. While crowds gathered and showed plenty of interest, the people showed a reluctance to yield to the Lord. There seemed to be a solid resistance to the Gospel message, and a lack of understanding of the claims of Christ.

Undaunted by the hardness of their hearts, Cecil began to minister to their physical needs in the tradition of Jesus and His apostles. She regularly distributed clothing to the families, especially the children. She showed the people how to make beds, how to equip and maintain their cabins, and how to exercise basic hygiene. Salvation Army Home

Leagues from all over the South made and donated garments to distribute among the families in Big Bend.

During the Christmas season, thousands of items reached the mountains from anonymous donors in the far reaches of the Southern Territory. Creature comforts and the simple conveniences of civilization slowly made the gospel message more palatable in Big Bend.

Although travel into Big Bend was difficult year-round, it was much harder during the frigid winters. On one return trip to her Maple Springs headquarters, the weather was so bitterly cold that Cecil couldn't get off her horse. When she finally did dismount, she could not walk, and two members of her family had to carry her inside.

PASTORAL COUNSELOR

Cecil not only had good medical skills, but she also put her counseling ability to use as well. On one occasion when a newborn baby became very ill, Cecil drove her to the hospital in Waynesville, where the baby died. The mother wanted to take the baby back to Big Bend, but hospital nurses said that would not be possible. Cecil succeeded in convincing the mother to give up the baby for burial. "She had a way of convincing people to do the right thing," a family member said.

Unlike many other mountain missions, the work at Big Bend did not last indefinitely. Because the farmland could not support the people, the forestry service eventually had to relocate all of the families according to a federal plan. One of two remaining groups included a family of four who had no road leading to their cabin. So, joining the county welfare officer, Cecil hiked four miles in the snow to bring the family down the mountain to their new home.

This family did not own enough household goods to even bother moving them. The parents and the welfare officer took what few personal items they had, and Cecil carried their two small girls. With one baby in a haversack on her back and another in her arms, she trudged down the mountain to the waiting car. The four-year old child, who had no shoes, was astounded at the sight of an automobile when they reached their destination. During the years that followed, Cecil continued to visit the one remaining family at Big Bend about once a year. The demands of the rest of the mission prevented her from going more often. On her final visit to the last family at Big Bend, the mother, who was blind, said her goodbyes to the captain and then added, "This is the first time anyone has read the Bible to me since your visit last year."

Even in a place as destitute as Big Bend, Cecil was not a strong advocate of government intervention. She believed that Christians should put their faith into action by helping each other voluntarily. If she went to a home and there was a need that she could fill, she would supply it. She touched countless lives, and fifty years after her death there are mountain people who remember her and still revere her name.

War Cry pages decorate a log cabin.

Chapter 8

The Depression and World War II

Early in his administration, President Franklin Roosevelt pointed to the South as the nation's "Number One Social Problem." The Salvation Army, which was struggling to cover its equipment and operating expenses throughout the country, was still in its infancy in the South when the region suddenly became paramount among the areas hit hardest by the Great Depression. Literally within the shadow of the Great Smoky Mountains, people were engulfed in a thick cloud of destitution and despair similar to the foggy mist that had given the area its name.

In Charlotte, N.C., the Army's divisional headquarters was mired in debt and fighting to sustain its supervisory and administrative programs. It could afford only minimal financial support for Cecil's projects during the Depression. World War II's mandatory rationing only added to the isolation of the Army's work in the mountains. Except for moral and in-kind support from divisional headquarters and the rest of the Southern territory, Cecil Brown had to operate independently.

Fortunately, she had wonderful support from Major Gilks, who had given her an opportunity to go to the mountains in the first place. He helped publicize the need for clothing and other supplies throughout the South, enabling a widespread positive response that lasted for many years.

The first three mountain missions – Shelton Laurel, Hurricane Creek, and Big Bend – had a Sunday School, held regular monthly worship services and conducted successful revival campaigns. They had suffered no major setbacks, and now the fourth location stood ready to be launched. Suddenly, Major Gilks received orders to leave Charlotte to take command of the Texas Division, and he had to leave behind the work he had helped Cecil to launch.

NEW LEADERSHIP

The appointment of a new divisional commander had raised concerns as to whether he would be able to understand the peculiar nature of the mountain work and continue to provide the necessary support. Fortunately, these fears vanished as soon as Lt. Colonel Alfred Tyler came to command the Carolinas and he showed an immediate interest in the mountain work.

During his stay, Major Gilks had made two inspection trips to the mountains, conducting meetings in Shelton Laurel and Hurricane Creek. Even though the mountaineers preferred "Miss Cecil" to the senior officers from Charlotte, they would never forget Major Gilks's car radio, which was still a conversation piece for many of the mountain folk.

After Colonel Tyler's welcome to the division, he immediately planned a trip to the mountains. The trip had to be timed according to the weather to ensure that the roads would be passable. Even before his first visit, Captain Brown had begun the fourth mission station without making an official announcement to her leaders. She simply sent a letter to divisional headquarters with the fourth location proudly set in type on her letterhead: Poplar Gap. The letterhead read: "Missionary Work of The Salvation Army, Western North Carolina. Mission Centers at Hurricane, N.C.; Shelton Laurel, N.C.; Big Bend, N.C.; Poplar Gap, N.C."

Actually, none of these locations could even be found on a state map. But if cartographers knew nothing about them, Cecil Brown had made them famous, at least in Salvation Army circles.

POPLAR GAP/LITTLE CREEK

On the surface, Poplar Gap looked like a carbon copy of the Army's missions at Shelton Laurel, Hurricane Creek, and Big Bend. Cecil held meetings in the schoolhouse, organized a Sunday School led by the locals, began a regular monthly worship meeting, and conducted a revival campaign. Even though the formula was identical, the fourth site had one key advantage.

While the first three communities had lacked a Christian foundation, Poplar Gap contained families who already knew the gospel, read their Bibles, prayed and practiced their faith. Because of this distinct difference, the work there grew so quickly that within a few years the congregation had its own meeting place built on a mountainside area known as Little Creek.

When the work at Little Creek started, meetings were conducted in a barn loft. One day Cecil wrote a letter informing headquarters that she needed another building because the farmer who had made his barn available needed his loft to store tobacco. Soon afterward, the corps family dedicated the facility that housed the Little Creek Chapel not far from the barn loft.

Little Creek stood for many years as a monument to the faith and works of the mountain families who had persevered in their devotion to God even when they lacked a place to worship. One man gave the land upon which the Little Creek Corps was built, while others donated their labor. In World War II figures, the Poplar Gap/Little Creek building cost about $1,800. The lovely chapel stood in a thicket of laurel and rhododendron bushes, about 500 feet up the mountain from the creek that bore its name. Many young men and boys in this church were converted and then later went off to war. Some of them died and they were buried in Africa and Italy far from their beloved mountains.

THE CHURCH IN THE WILDWOOD

Major Glenna West remembers her first Sunday in 1945 as a youth at the Little Creek Corps. "We lived at the end of the road, and our neighbors invited us to go to church. We walked down to their house, and they took us up a winding trail to the road, where we were joined by a lot of other people going to Little Creek.

"We got up there, and I almost went home before I went inside! The only church I'd ever seen that wasn't white was brick. And I couldn't believe that we were going to a brown church. When we got inside, and Major Brown and Captain Colton came in, I looked at those horrible-looking uniforms, and I thought, *What have I gotten myself into!* I sat on one of those pews and only stayed there because I really didn't know the way home.

"All the people crowded into the small room, huddling around Cecil as though she were the Commander-in-Chief," Glenna said. "My two sisters and I were standing off to the side. We were clueless as to what was going on or even who this lady was." Then she remembers Cecil looking around and saying, "Well, who are our new friends?"

"That made me feel good. Cecil literally pulled my family into that corps' circle of love.

"There was something else shocking about that first Sunday. I remember that they let a teenager read the Scripture! I thought, *Well, if they are going to let kids my age read from the Bible, I'll keep coming!* So I did," she said.

VACATION BIBLE SCHOOL

Florence Wall played a key role in the Little Creek mission while she served as one of Cecil's lieutenants. "I conducted Vacation Bible School (VBS) at Little Creek," she said. "I stayed there while doing VBS until just before school reopened. We used to perform Bible skits that the children loved. In one skit, young David needed a harp to play, so I asked the children what we could use for a harp. One boy suggested that we could use a dustpan! A dustpan? 'Yes,' he said, 'we can put some strings on this dustpan and pretend it is a harp.' The kids loved to use their imagination."

Another skit featured the Wise Men arriving in Bethlehem to visit the Baby Jesus who was asleep in His stable. The Wise Men needed staffs, but the kids called them "canes." So Florence asked what they could use for staffs. Some of the kids said that they would bring something the next day. What they brought the next day were broomsticks!

"I did a commencement service and we always had some refreshments for them because they had to travel from so far away. Anything we had for them, they appreciated – cupcakes, juice, candy – whatever," Florence said.

"Cecil would often come and she sometimes brought visitors to observe the work. Once she brought a college professor, and later she told me that he marveled at the fact that we were able to do so much with so little. We had fun doing so many things with these children, even if we did have to improvise."

"My quarters at Little Creek were very small," Florence said. "I lived there by myself. I slept in the back room of the mission station where I could hear the creek. I loved hearing that creek, and I didn't mind being alone. I knew the neighbors. I couldn't see them but I knew they were there. I took books to read, I planned the children's programs and even baked cookies for them. So time flew!"

Lieutenant Doris McQuay, who served only six months with Cecil Brown, left her appointment in the mountains with a profound respect for Cecil. She still relates fond memories of her welcome meeting at the Little Creek Corps. Cecil's nephew, Mickey, drove her there in the jeep. When they arrived, he lowered the top rail of a split-rail fence so Doris could easily step over, and they walked up to the little brown church in the wildwood. When they went into the corps, about 20 people greeted her. It was a brand-new experience for a city girl to see the separation of the sexes.

"I remember the first time I saw Little Creek, I remember thinking to myself, *Well where are all these people going to be coming from* – because there were no houses that I could see! But then, here they'd all be coming, walking miles from their homes to the corps," Doris said.

"I met the lady who was going to introduce me and also lead the meeting. A young boy played a cornet that provided the music for the service. He had been taught to play by Brigadier Lillian Blackburn when she was stationed up there many years before me. They sang songs that night I had never heard of, out of a songbook with shaped notes that I had never seen before, either.

"I was in charge of the Little Creek Corps and Lieutenant Marjorie Key was in charge of the Maple Spring Corps, where we both lived. After lunch each Sunday, she and I would go to the Shelton Laurel Corps to hold a meeting there. Cecil would start out very early each Sunday morning and go to her three corps. I went with her several times, and it was a real treat and a great blessing to watch her conduct the meetings and interact with her people. She really knew how to reach them with the Gospel."

When the building needed painting, Doris continued, the corps leaders had to improvise. "We made our own paint by combining old motor oil, creosote and another ingredient. They had the service station save the old motor oil for their paint. They'd mix these things together, but they wouldn't let me paint, because I was a woman even though I was the corps officer. There used to be a tiny house behind Little Creek, but nobody was living there. It had a little kitchen, so I'd go in there and fix a meal for everyone while they painted.

"The mixture they painted with actually stained the wood, like a redwood. I think the last time I saw that building it was still that reddish-brown tint," she said.

Brigadier James Henry described the interior of the Little Creek Corps with its walls made of fine chestnut wood. "It was worth a lot of money because you could make fine furniture out of wood like that," he said. "And the ceiling was solid cherry. It was a treasure!"

VIP VISITS

Colonel Tyler followed up his introduction to the new Army corps with an amusing report to the territorial commander. "We had an enjoyable trip to Poplar Gap and Little Creek. If you could see the mountain climbing we had to do, and if you can visualize Captain Brown in a Chevrolet coupe with all of the baggage piled in the rumble seat climbing up a mountain road where the rains had washed deep gullies and bumping over rocks, you can get a picture of what we experienced. Captain Brown is a regular Jehu when it comes to driving up the mountains. As soon as she gets to a straight stretch, she steps on the gas and we hold on for dear life!

"When we reached Poplar Gap, we found the schoolhouse full. They were singing when we went in. A tall mountaineer served as the song leader, pitching his voice two or three times until he got the right pitch and then he started the singing. Major Willard Evans' concertina was quite an attraction. They had never seen anything like that before at Poplar Gap."

Another special tour involved the Southern Territorial Commander, Commissioner Ernest Pugmire and Major Sidney Cox. Two of the Army's most dignified leaders got a taste of rustic ministry in the mountains. They came for one weekend and they had to ride horses to reach several of the mission stations they inspected. The corps buildings were tiny one-room structures that doubled as schools during the week and as churches on Sundays. Cecil's biggest problem was finding a place for the commissioner and Major Cox to sleep. They stayed three nights in her humble quarters. Commissioner Pugmire slept on one side of the room and Major Cox on the other side, with a curtain in between. Cecil went down the mountain to stay with friends.

BRAVING THE BITTER COLD

By now, the effort required to serve the four established stations had drained most of Cecil's energy. Every wintry onslaught made the burden more difficult. Snow often blocked roads for as long as two weeks at a time. Although the mountain inhabitants were used to it, the captain worried about finishing her work faithfully and on schedule.

The car that Cecil drove was only useful up to a point. Whenever bad weather came, whether rain or snow, she had to travel by horseback or on foot. Actually, she preferred walking or riding horseback because she could enter areas where her car was unable to go.

"No road was too long, no hill too high, no creek too wide, no day too icy or too hot, for her to take off on foot or on horseback or by jeep, to visit the sick or comfort the sorrowing, to tend the newborn, or bury the dead," the *War Cry* reported.

A less vigorous woman would not have survived those winters, let alone the heavy year-round demands of the work. One March she made an ambitious trip to all four churches – a total of 75 miles by horseback. With each spring she renewed her effort to visit families she could not reach during the winter. The people always received her warmly and eagerly awaited better weather when she could return more often.

During one of Cecil's early spring trips an untimely blizzard buried the highlands. People said it was the heaviest snow they'd had in nearly 50 years. Four-foot drifts blocked the roads, and the ensuing thaw wreaked havoc by creating muddy quagmires and washing away roads. Once, on her way back to her headquarters, a downed tree blocked the path of her horse. She had to summon help to clear the way back down the mountains to her home. To make matters worse, her mouth ached from the pain of a recent tooth extraction. Throughout these trials and tribulations, Cecil savored her accomplishments for God, and she looked ahead to future expansion of the mission work.

Official opening of Little Creek Corps

Chapter 9

Courting the Media

With her work firmly established, Cecil was now working and visiting in a wider area of western North Carolina and eastern Tennessee. In addition to maintaining the four mission stations, many churches and schoolhouses called on her and asked her to tell the story of The Salvation Army in her beloved mountains.

Radio and Newspapers

She learned how to use the media to her advantage, especially radio and newspapers. Brigadier James Henry, who was serving in 1938 as a young officer in Ashland, Kentucky, turned on his radio one night to find the popular program, "*We The People Speak,*" sponsored by Gulf Oil Company.

"I heard the announcer say, 'Captain Cecil Brown of The Salvation Army...' And my ears perked up, because I had heard of her, too. He said, 'We're going to interview Captain Brown, and she runs the mountain work in western North Carolina.'

"So they started talking to Cecil, and I remember that it wasn't a long interview. I understand, however, that the Gulf Oil Company went all out to get mountain people to the radio station in Asheville, North Carolina. They even sent those long stretch-limousines as far up into the mountains as they could to bring some of those people to town. There were limousines lined up back-to-back. It must have been something to see – can you imagine those limousines going around those curves?

"I remember Cecil saying as the radio host was closing the program, 'Aren't you going to let us sing our mountain Christmas Carol?' And he said, 'Oh, yes, by all means!'

"She evidently had a string band with her. They started to sing *Beautiful Star Of Bethlehem*. That was the end of the program. Later on I found out that the Gulf Oil Company gave her a beautiful new jeep and other stuff for her work."

Major Doris McQuay met Cecil on her way to New York City for a nationally televised program that would tell about her work in the mountains. Cecil had stopped in Baltimore to speak at a citywide Army function held at the Patterson Park Corps.

"I was a soldier at that corps, and I remember sitting there wide-eyed as she talked about her work," Doris said. "I never dreamed that one day I would be stationed with her."

Brigadier Dorothy Langston remembers flattering portraits of Cecil and her work that were painted by the media. "On the Sunday in the mid-1930s when she arrived in the mountains, the paper did a full-page story. When she died more than 20 years later, the coverage was just as loving. It marked the passing of someone who was truly exceptional."

As a constant guest on local and nationwide radio programs, Cecil became an instant celebrity. One newspaper reporter had heard that the Army was raising funds to send needy mountain children to summer camp, so he interviewed her and then wrote an inspiring editorial that prompted generous donations for a number of camp scholarships.

An Inquisitive Reporter

Readers' Digest also expressed interest in the Army's work and sent a reporter to the mountains who aroused Cecil's suspicions. Leery of the reporter's motives, Cecil concluded that she intended to portray mountaineers as stupid hillbillies and to make fun of them. She later said that the woman had smoked in bed and had burned a hole in a brand-new mattress. Then the reporter inquired about the moonshine business and asked to see a still. She had planned to stay a week or two, but Cecil kicked her out after three days. She threw her off the mountain, saying, "Go – get your suitcase and leave. Don't come back, and I don't care if you write that story or not!"

She paid a price for her rashness, however, when the reporter returned to New York and complained to Army leadership there. Cecil received a harsh letter from headquarters accusing her of ruining the relationship between *Readers' Digest* and The Salvation Army.

Cecil published a newsletter called the *Mountain Circle News* – later on it was known as *Mountain Life* – which was typed and mimeographed by one of her assistants. She delivered it throughout the mountains and beyond, to keep people aware of what was going on.

Though she skillfully used the media to raise money for the work, her chief source of joy was in the people who were saved. During the first year, more than 130 people made a profession of faith, including 30 people who were enrolled as Salvation Army soldiers. In addition, changes occurred in the lives and conduct of hundreds of others whom she considered "on the cusp" of making a full surrender to God. Even when the influence of the Gospel didn't appear outwardly to save a soul, Cecil could still see its impact for good.

NICKELS AND DIMES

Cecil prayed for a structure that would serve as a corps, her headquarters and her living quarters. Unlike other missionaries, she had no home church to subsidize her work. So she followed the good old Army custom of soliciting nickels and dimes in a tambourine. This had worked in many other Salvation Army ventures around the world – why not in the mountains?

Such an approach, however, placed more demands on her time and energy, which were already stretched thin. Not a week passed without her visiting towns and villages, along with her tambourine, all the way from the Tennessee state line to Georgia and South Carolina. One week she would take one route, the next, another. Using this system, she covered all of her territory in a single month.

Major William Range, the financial secretary for the Carolinas at the time, reported that the work in the Smoky Mountains cost a total of $1,098.15 annually. According to Major Range's financial statement, divisional headquarters had advanced only $377.50. The remainder had been laboriously collected in small donations from the length and breadth of Cecil's domain in western North Carolina.

Cecil knew that it took a lot of nickels and dimes to make a thousand dollars. But it also took frugality. If the money had come more easily, perhaps the work might not have been as lucrative. At any rate, real sacrifices went into the income and expenses of the mission in those first years.

Commissioner Samuel Logan Brengle sought to aid the mountain work through his friend, Senator Royal S. Copeland of New York. The commissioner expressed confidence that the Army could obtain a $5,000 federal grant through the help of Senator Copeland. Now that the New Deal was firmly in place and billions of dollars were being pumped into the economy, he hoped that Cecil Brown's good work would be endorsed. But it was not to be.

A disappointed commissioner appealed to Colonel Tyler. "Last week, I asked Royal Copeland, our Senator from New York, to provide funds to feed and clothe the poor children in the mountains of Carolina and Tennessee. He says that there are no public funds for this. I would like, if you have no objection, to lay this work before my old friend, S. Parks Cadman, with a request that he broadcast a statement of Cecil's work and her needs." Although Commissioner Brengle failed to obtain any government funds, knowledge of Cecil's work began to grow through radio and newspaper coverage.

On the air in Asheville

Chapter 10

Stretched to the Limit

Salvation Army leaders in New York, Atlanta and Charlotte all took an interest in the success and the problems of the mission. Because of the value placed on her work, in 1939 Cecil received a promotion from Captain to Adjutant at the age of 32.

While Army leaders talked about raising thousands of dollars to support her, it was the mountain people who supplied the most practical assistance. Her soldiers, family and friends decided to build a cottage for her next to the Shelton Laurel schoolhouse.

THE ARCHITECT

Suddenly Cecil needed to add the role of architect to her long list of talents. Many pioneer women before her had drawn the plans for a new house like the one she and her neighbors were about to build. Why couldn't she? It would be a simple structure, and she knew exactly what the project would involve.

The coming of spring had opened up the roads and trails and cleared the forests of snow, allowing the men around Shelton Laurel to cut enough young pine trees to build a small log house for their pastor. This collective effort gave them a chance to show their appreciation above and beyond the $25 contribution that they were paying regularly. Still, most of the mountaineers had trouble coming to terms with The Salvation Army's basic regulations on property matters.

CORPORATE CHANNELS

After many years of owning property around the world, The Salvation Army had developed a sound policy that oversaw the acquisition of land, the designing of structures and the construction of Army facilities. No one could commit the Army corporation to a building project or accept real estate donations without first following a well-defined and proven procedure. The property board in Atlanta, however, seemed light years away from the mountains, where the people's only desire was to build a more convenient house for Cecil.

In a move around Army bureaucracy, Cecil informed her divisional commander of her plans to build a two-room house out of pine logs, and of her hope to move in within two weeks. She quickly sent a photo to headquarters of the modest little house, which had a stone path leading up to the front door and rhododendrons lining the entranceway. The basic description called for stained brown logs, with green shutters and white doors and windows. Since no mountain cabin in Shelton Laurel had running water, Cecil failed to mention that the house would lack modern conveniences. The entire cost for her new quarters was $8.50!

IRATE LEADERSHIP

After the Southern *War Cry* printed a copy of the photo, Commissioner Ernest Pugmire, then the territorial commander, realized that the property board had not yet received a formal proposal. He promptly fired off an inquiry letter to the Carolinas divisional commander, and the colonel in Charlotte replied that he knew about the house but had not been consulted about the legal rights of The Salvation Army. The members of the property board grew incensed over the acquisition of unapproved real estate, but they stood helpless, and a formal deed soon arrived at headquarters.

Cecil's new abode was just one of several jurisdictional conflicts with the Army over the years. Increasingly, the upper echelon had begun to realize that the mountain undertaking lacked a precedent within the framework of the parent organization. A great deal of misunderstanding arose, and better communication had to be developed before the work could be fully implemented. Still, the top decision makers knew that Cecil's work reflected her zeal, devotion, and dedication – as well as her personal idiosyncrasies.

PERSONAL INSPECTION

Cecil's detour around official Army channels incited the commissioner to begin a personal inspection of the work under his command. The divisional commander also realized the need to become more intimately acquainted with the strategy in the mountains. Although the spirit of this ministry mirrored advances in the early Church as seen in the Acts of the Apostles, its agenda did not easily fit into the *Orders and Regulations for Officers of The Salvation Army.*

Salvation Army leaders reached two key decisions as an indirect result of the house incident at Shelton Laurel. First, Commissioner Pugmire would visit the Army's now-extensive work in the Smokies. Secondly, Cecil would receive an opportunity to tell her story to Army officers assembled before a territorial council.

DONATIONS

When the Southern Territory met in Atlanta, officers from the large towns and cities were bemoaning the decline in Sunday School attendance. As they discussed how to sustain the interest of city children, Cecil sat bemused waiting for her turn to speak. Then she eagerly told them about Hurricane Creek, Max Patch and a half dozen other communities whose inhabitants had crowded into borrowed schoolhouses and shacks.

"I was just thinking," Cecil said, "how these men have their buildings and no people – and I have people and no buildings! Now, if somehow we could make a swap . . ." When she sat down total silence fell on the crowd, followed by a murmur of voices. Finally one officer jumped up and said, "Let's give that girl a building! I'll give $100!" Within fifteen minutes the officers had raised $2600 for her. "I carried the building back in an envelope," she said triumphantly.

Once an acre of land had been donated, her father and her brothers, Fletcher and John, built a beautiful T-shaped structure made of rock and hemlock that held 250 people. The citadel became her headquarters for many years.

Brigadier James Henry explained how quickly that part of the project got off the ground. "She had her father, who was an excellent carpenter, and her brothers, who were also carpenters – she had all of them working, and before you could say 'Jack Robinson' there was the Maple Springs Citadel.

"Actually, while they were building it, some Presbyterians had a church just across the river, and they came to Cecil and said, 'we're moving out – we want to give you our church.' So she took it and started holding meetings there, until one night it caught fire and burned down."

In three short years, Cecil had progressed from a 6 x 6 foot trailer attached to the back of her car, to a two-room log cabin built by the people of Shelton Laurel, to a modern building just outside of Waynesville. From this center, she could carry out her work in Waynesville, Shelton Laurel, Poplar Gap, and Hurricane Creek.

God had blessed Cecil with the ability to persuade an audience by using eloquent simplicity and sincerity. In 1948, a *War Cry* story captured the compelling power of her voice. "When the Territorial Staff Band strikes up a couple of impromptu numbers, when an extra collection yields showers of dollar bills, and when enthusiasm reaches a veritable spontaneous combustion, we are witnessing a demonstration that must have been sparked by an unusual person. Major Brown commanded the attention of her audience from the moment she started to speak and she held them entranced as she gave a breathtaking account of her work."

Burnout

The Salvation Army seemed content with the progress of the work and the waging of the war on sin. But this ministry had grown so quickly that rules had to be strictly enforced; otherwise, the maverick missionary in charge threatened to become a "loose cannon." At the very least, everyday problems needed sympathetic attention from the top levels.

Almost single-handedly, Cecil had responsibility for managing the overall mission. She had stoically borne the burdens of preaching at several sites, crossing rugged mountain trails in all kinds of weather, and serving as a social worker, doctor, lawyer, taxi driver, farmer, friend, and a Good Samaritan. She admitted that the physical strain of directing a blossoming ministry, "besides the care of all the churches," had brought her to the breaking point. Now her superiors were adding another layer of stress to her job by insisting that she tow the bureaucratic line.

Cecil needed a partner to share the responsibility of administration and care for her people. But who else would be willing to make the sacrifices necessary for this type of work? The training college could take raw cadets and mold them into officers, but no classroom course could prepare a Salvation Army cadet to become another Cecil Brown.

Cecil took the matter to the two most sympathetic listeners she knew: her Heavenly Father and her divisional commander. Overwrought by physical weariness and growing anxiety, she had a more informal relationship with the Lord than she did with Colonel Tyler. She prayed with characteristic bluntness, "Now, Lord, if you don't get me some help, I'm a-goin' to quit." To her divisional commander, she sent a more formal, restrained request for an assistant.

Communication with divisional headquarters seemed to move at a snail's pace. Colonel Tyler said that certain officers might be persuaded to renounce their comfortable appointments and accept the rigors of mountain work. But Cecil now harbored a growing distrust of the higher echelon, and she hesitated to accept any assistant appointed by her divisional commander.

THELMA COLTON

Meanwhile, in answer to her prayer, God had placed His hand upon a girl who turned out to be much more than an assistant. Thelma Colton became a coequal partner in Cecil Brown's beloved mission. In Thelma, God had prepared a girl in heart and spirit who would make a contribution that even Cecil could not duplicate.

When Cecil received the first letter from Thelma postmarked from faraway Texas, she had her doubts. Maybe that is understating it – she nearly threw the letter away. But something made her read the letter again.

Thelma wrote that she had spoken with a Salvationist friend who had just returned from a territorial event in Atlanta after hearing Cecil speak. Thelma had listened to her friend relate the story of the Mountain Mission. What a story it was! Could she, an unknown girl from Texas, come up and help?

Cecil, always the pragmatist, feared that the girl from Texas saw only the romanticism of this unique type of work. She wrote back to Thelma, hoping to strip away her idealism about working in the mountains. She left nothing to her imagination: "If you can live with me in crowded quarters, wear cotton hose and low heel shoes, eat mountain fare, have no guarantee of a salary, walk long miles in all kinds of weather, and like it – Come!"

This was not much of an invitation or a welcome, but at least it was honest. Thelma turned out to be what some of the mountain people liked to call a "girl preacher." From her first mountain sermon to a gathering in a Poplar Gap barn loft, she seemed to have found her destiny. Meanwhile, Cecil quietly rejoiced that the Lord, and not the divisional commander, had answered her prayers.

Cecil saw Thelma as a person whom God had prepared for this work in His own way. She was not looking for romance in the mountains after all. As David's heart joined with Jonathan's in the Old Testament, so did the hearts of Cecil Brown and Thelma Colton. Their initial meeting marked the beginning of a beautiful friendship, and the two women made a perfect team. But how did God actually prepare Thelma to work with Cecil?

She had been born in Michigan, educated in Florida, and raised by a spiritual mother. Mrs. Colton could not afford to dress her five children "suitably" for Sunday School and church. She decided that since they could not attend a "fancy" Sunday School, she would start her own neighborhood school. Eventually it developed into a mission, which Thelma, at age 15, helped to run, first out of loyalty to her mother, and later to show her devotion to God. Thelma had known about the Lord but had not yet experienced His precious presence in her life. Over the course of time, she did.

Following her conversion she attended Bible School and then she trained for fulltime Christian work. She graduated from a Christian college in Los Angeles, returned to her family's mission – which had been renamed the "Gospel Tabernacle" – and she agreed to become their assistant pastor.

The following year, her career as a "girl preacher" saw a meteoric rise after she received a promotion to senior pastor. Other churches had heard about her power in the pulpit, and requests for a speaker started to pour from various denominations.

Thelma met The Salvation Army in Spartanburg, S.C., preaching a revival campaign there, in Raleigh, N.C., and in several other divisional corps. She loved preaching in the corps, where she believed she had found a great field for soul winning. She also admired the Army's ability to attract people who felt uncomfortable in other places of worship.

Then she had a meeting with Lt. Colonel William Gilks, Cecil's former divisional commander, which was serendipitous. He briefed her on Cecil's work, and she was permanently hooked.

Colonel Gilks, however, wanted Thelma to pursue a career as an Army evangelist. She listened, but she began to hear the clarion call of God to go to the mountains and help Cecil. Thus, unwittingly, Colonel Gilks continued to support the ongoing development of the mountain effort.

If Thelma had any doubts about her ability to preach, they quickly evaporated once she stood before the congregation at Poplar Gap. Amid the solitude and the vastness of the Great Smoky Mountains, she knew this was where God wanted her to be.

With almost unrestrained joy, Cecil wrote to her divisional commander: "I am now in a meeting at Poplar Gap with Miss Thelma Colton. Our crowds have been large and the time seems ripe for a real revival. Miss Colton is the best revivalist I've ever had. Her messages are wonderful! People are coming from miles around to hear her."

Cecil ended her letter by expressing hope that the people would donate enough money to pay her new assistant a weekly salary of ten dollars.

At work with Salvation Army leaders

Chapter 11

Marriage or Career?

If we accept the premise of Sigmund Freud, then love and work constitute the cornerstones of our humanity. Yet during Cecil's era and up until the 1970's, American society tended to devalue the importance of work in a woman's life. In the United States, the vast majority of women married, raised children, and became homemakers. A minority of women who worked outside the home generally did so because of economic necessity. It was highly unusual for a woman to choose a full-time career over marriage and family. Moreover, the idea that a woman could both work and raise a family was still unheard of in American society. So, given the cultural climate, in most conversations about Cecil Brown, the question invariably arose: Why did she remain single? There is certainly no shortage of theories.

During the rare times that she spoke of her private life, she confided only in those who were closest to her. People who knew her well said that before she joined The Salvation Army she was deeply in love, but for some reason, she never married. Perhaps because of that disappointing end, she never opened her heart again.

Blanche Lowe said that, "Cecil Brown never got married, but I know for a fact that she was in love at one time. I think whoever that was, was not faithful to her. Something happened. That was her one true love, I guess. She didn't like to talk about it.

"I don't know if she ever missed being married, but she turned that to an advantage. Many mountain people thought that a woman had no business being a preacher and that a woman should let her husband do the preaching. I remember Cecil would say to people (about being a single female preacher): 'Well, I'm not married – I don't have a husband to leave that to! It's me! I'm the only one!'"

In The Salvation Army an officer may only marry another officer. Therefore, even if Cecil had married "within the ranks," the couple could have been asked to serve anywhere in the Southern Territory – when all along her heart would have been with her people in the mountains.

THE SERENADE

At the training college in Atlanta, one male cadet actively pursued her as a potential partner. Cecil's dorm room was on the second floor, and as the young man stood on ground level below her window, he started singing *Carolina Moon Keep Shining*. Unmoved, she quickly opened her window and poured a pail of ice water on the poor fellow! Thus ended that romance.

JUNE AND REESE

June Brown, Cecil's niece and the daughter of Fletcher Brown, believed that Cecil only opposed marriage when it seemed to threaten the work of the mission. When one of her aides began to show an interest in a young man, she would try to discourage the relationship. With her niece, however, she showed much more flexibility. Reese Ferguson showed an interest in June, and while Cecil eyed him with caution, over time his contribution to her work eventually won her approval. Cecil performed the wedding ceremony for June and Reese in front of the fireplace at Maple Springs.

"Reese and I met about the time I was going to school at Fines Creek," June said. "He is four years older than me, and he had already graduated. I saw him coming to the school for programs and things, but I got to know him when he came to the corps at Maple Springs. He'd walk out there from his home eight miles away. Sometimes he rode an old horse his family had.

"Aunt Cecil didn't approve of him at first. In fact, she didn't approve of anyone for me to begin with. But we did our courting in the dining room there at Maple Springs, under her watchful eye. We brought some chairs over there to sit in. But by nine o'clock he had to be gone!"

June said that Reese would accompany her and Cecil to meetings at the Bonnie Hill Corps. Many times he would return with them to Maple Springs and then he would have to walk the eight miles home.

"Once in a while, Aunt Cecil would say to me, 'You can take Reese home in the Army's jeep,'" June said. "But I had a certain number of minutes to go to Fines Creek, then back to Maple Springs. So there was no time for hanky-panky! In time she came to accept him. But she would always call him, 'That Ferguson!'"

BEST WISHES

Often Cecil would attend the weddings of family and friends to share her best wishes for the newlyweds. One such bride was Thelma Hall. Thelma served as a corps soldier for about five years, and she became Cecil's aide for nearly a year before she left for The Salvation Army's training college in Atlanta. She never returned to the mountains, but Cecil did attend her wedding.

"When I got married in 1944 she came to my wedding in Winston-Salem," Thelma said. "She seemed happy for me and even took up a love offering of $15 from the mountain people. Her main concern was to see that I amounted to something. She wanted so much to instill something in me that I needed – values in life.

"When I was still single and working with her, she would kid me about one of the young men in the corps. I would call on him to read the scripture most of the time because I liked the way he read. Cecil would say to me, 'Thelma, what's this about every Sunday morning you're asking Wendell to read the scripture?' She kidded me as if I had an eye on him. I didn't, but one of the girls did marry him later on after I had left for the training college," she said.

CROSSING THE LINE

Others voiced their belief that Cecil had discouraged them from marrying. Major Florence Wall arrived at the Mountain Mission in 1947, and she stayed until her marriage to Lieutenant Jack Brewer. Her husband was one of the few successful suitors among Cecil's lieutenants. "I knew she didn't like me at all!" Jack said. "When Cecil looked at me, I could feel the daggers shooting toward me."

Florence agreed with Jack's assessment of the situation. "She didn't like Jack too much because she kind of felt that he was taking me away from the work at the Mountain Mission. She heard he had a wreck once on his way up the mountain to see me. She said that it served him right, because he didn't tell us he was coming!

"That wasn't a very nice thing for her to say, but I wasn't all that surprised. She may not have liked him, but she didn't dwell on it because I guess she knew it wouldn't do much good.

"The lieutenants often wondered if she had once been disappointed in love. We understood that at one time she had been engaged to be married, and that he died or something happened that prevented the marriage. But she never gave us a hard time as far as our own personal relationships – not too much, anyway!"

Major Mildred Kirby, another lieutenant who married soon after leaving the mountains, noted that sometimes Cecil tried to play matchmaker for her lieutenants. One male officer who visited the mountains seemed to be on the lookout for a wife. "He was not my type, and he couldn't drive," Mildred explained. "I thought, well, who wants to marry a man who can't drive? Cecil thought he had his eye on me, and in this case, she was encouraging it. I think she was trying to fix me up with him, but I didn't want him. That made her mad."

Mildred said that she had neither seen nor heard of the officer again until she and Major Harry Foden were stationed at the Chattanooga East Lake Corps, before their retirement. "We went to Officers Councils, and there he was. I went up to him and said, 'Hey, let's get us a jeep and go for a ride up in the mountains!' He just died laughing," she said.

Trust

Major Jean Frese related an incident that manifested Cecil's reticence toward strangers, especially in matters of the heart. "One day a man came working on the road – he was a surveyor," Jean said. "He knew Cecil was a good shot. So he got a target out and a rifle, and he said, 'Let's practice.'

"So they did, and she hit the bull's eye every time. When he shot, he missed even the target, let alone the bull's eye. I had never shot a gun in my life. I at least hit the board, but I missed the target," Jean said.

"The mountain people back then were different from the way they are today. He just wanted to see her shoot, because he knew she was good. I took my jacket off and he held it for me. When he did that, Cecil looked a bit concerned. And when I hit the target, he went to hug me. But he took one look at Cecil, and he just handed me my jacket, gently dropping it on my shoulders.

"I think she realized he didn't mean anything – he was just being nice. After he left, she said to me, 'People aren't trying to take advantage of you or anything, are they? They just love you for you! It's just wholesome.'"

GENDER EQUALITY

Brigadier Dorothy Langston offered a glimpse into the perception of Cecil held by the opposite sex. Dorothy, herself a recipient of the Order of the Founder, spoke frankly about the reverence men had for her. "From what I could tell, men respected her, and she respected them but at the same time she could speak to a man as strongly as men spoke to each other."

"She was an equal to men in every respect," Dorothy said. "There was an aura about her that commanded a sense of awe, even among the men."

At least into her thirties, Cecil may have had opportunities for romance. In a 1936 diary entry she mentioned receiving a Valentine card from "R," but no one could identify who sent the card. Other diary entries lamented her loneliness. Phrases such as "my lonely room" or "went home alone" seeped into her writings at the end of days that were especially hectic and tiresome. Clearly, her passion for the work of the Salvation Army consumed her brief life. It could almost be called "her destiny."

Such is love's sacrifice.

A cup of tea at Maple Springs, 1949

Chapter 12

Tales of the Wild

In 1938, Cecil and her first assistants had to adapt to primitive living conditions in Maple Springs. They had little or no furniture, and Cecil slept on a cot with a straw mattress. Before heating equipment was installed, the officers used two metal oil barrels. They cut a hole in the side of each one for the door and fastened the piece taken out of the hole with metal hinges. There was a hole in the top for a pipe and a small hole in the bottom to provide a draft. "They make very effective stoves," the War Cry joked.

For Major Glenna West, a healthy sense of humor – if not a positive spin – made the housing hardships tolerable.

"We had a cabin at Maple Springs. There were no telephones and no electricity. We had to chop wood to burn in the fireplace. At least we never had to worry about paying utility bills and having the power turned off!"

Poignantly holding a photo of the first officers' quarters, which depicted no more than a box with a door, she said, "I think a copy of this photo should be sent to every newly commissioned captain, to remind them of how hard things were then."

Florence Wall recalled that the lack of resources did not seem to matter to the officers. Oil lamps were used prior to electricity, and they had to be handled with extreme caution. If a fire broke out, the only way to fight it was to draw water from the spring. A cottage could easily become engulfed by the time any appreciable amount of water could be brought to douse the blaze.

FIRE!

"One Sunday, I was stoking up the pot-bellied stove," Florence said. "It was very cold outside, but the stove was red hot. Even the stovepipe leading up to the wall looked red. I didn't know what to do. So I got a bucket of water, and opened the door of that stove with a potholder, and I threw that water onto the fire."

Cinders and hot coals blew back at her and literally knocked her over. The corps people later said that only a miracle kept her from getting hurt or even killed. "It just singed my eyebrows," she said. "Somebody told me that my guardian angel must have been on duty that day because it was a miracle I didn't burn down the corps and me with it!"

On another cold morning, Florence encountered a different kind of problem. The bathrooms were on top of a hill, and the ground was so icy, she could not make her way to the top. "I kept sliding back! I was in full uniform and the other lieutenants were waiting for me. I got so frustrated – I finally cried out to God to help me. I felt so small and He seemed so big at that moment. I finally made it up and back!"

A RELUCTANT CORPSE

One of the funniest anecdotes shared by several of Cecil's lieutenants concerned a corpse missing from a funeral near Hot Springs. Cecil and her assistants had arrived at the chapel along with the rest of the congregation. The only person absent was the "guest of honor."

The mortician, who brought the body from nearby Rockingham, was completely unfamiliar with the mountains, and he grew hopelessly lost. He drove the hearse around for hours trying to decipher the directions he had been given. Meanwhile, Lieutenant Wall had begun to play the piano while Cecil reviewed her notes alone in the back room.

Hours passed, Florence had played every gospel song she knew at least twice, and still no body arrived. People started to grow restless. Women were sitting in the pews trying to quiet their children, while many of the men stood outside smoking and waiting.

By five o'clock, one of the lieutenants informed Cecil that the mortician was lost. She dismissed the crowd and informed them that when the body was located, the service would reconvene. The next morning the hearse arrived, and she preached to a crowd that had shrunken noticeably. Her lieutenants could not attend because of other duties around the mission. Cecil asked the mortician, who was already in a bad mood, if he could pray. "Not out loud, I can't," he said.

"Well, you won't be any help to me," she said. Then she asked the few attendees there, "Can anybody here sing?" A couple of people said, "Yes, we can get some songs together." That was the extent of the service.

When the funeral ended, Cecil explained to the mortician that the cemetery was located on top of the mountain. The hearse could only go so far, and then the coffin would have to be placed in her jeep to travel further. After that, it would have to be carried up the final hundred yards to the gravesite. The mortician was so angry that he left as soon as the final "amen" was pronounced. Cecil loved that story so much that years later whenever she told it tears of laughter would fill her eyes.

A CLANDESTINE BURIAL

Another unusual funeral took place at the infamous Big Bend. A woman had died, the family did not want to bury her, and everyone had gotten drunk. Thelma Colton distracted the women in one room of the house (the men were not a problem because they had all passed out!) – while Cecil enlisted three Civilian Conservation Corps employees to help her carry the body to the cemetery and conduct the burial before anyone realized it was gone. A riot nearly occurred, but Cecil finally convinced the grieving family that their loved one deserved a decent burial.

On one occasion the women were picking berries near Big Bend. The logging company had abandoned the area, removed the doors and windows from the homes, and left their foundations behind. One home had a hollowed tree stump in front, which was ideal for building a cooking fire. After a tiring day of hard work in the hot sun, everyone had retired there for the night. Cecil had a mattress on the floor, and the lieutenants spent the night on cots. Peewee, their dog, slept under one of the cots.

During the night, one of the lieutenants awoke to the sound of Peewee growling. She reached down to pat him and found that his hair was standing up. Something had obviously scared him. Then she heard the rattlesnake. As she held her breath, the snake apparently slithered out the door and into the night.

The next morning, she asked the others: "Did anyone hear a rat-tlesnake during the night?" Cecil confirmed it. Yes, it was a snake, and it had passed by the major's head on the way out.

Dorothy Langston recalled that Cecil often encountered snakes, bears, and once even a cougar, but that wild animals never alarmed her. "I don't think she ever took a gun with her, but she had a whip," Dorothy said. "She kept that whip handy in case a wild animal got too close. I don't think she had any fear of any person, man or beast." Dorothy could remember only one instance when Cecil got hurt. While traveling on her visitation rounds, she climbed up a rocky ledge and fell and broke her arm.

Home Pest Control

Jean Frese described the unorthodox way that Cecil and her family would rid their house of pests. "Major Brown took me down to Hurri-cane Creek where she was raised," Jean said. "We would scrub the floors with lye soap and that would bring out the mice, rats and snakes. They'd fly out on both sides of the house. Major would be on one side, and her nephew Mickey would be on the other side – and as the vermin came out, they'd shoot them!"

Purloined Property

Jean continued to relate how Cecil dealt with another kind of unwanted guest – thieves. Noticing supplies missing from the springhouse, she had firmly resolved to catch the culprits. One day as her group left for town, she retraced her steps and waited with a loaded rifle upstairs in the Maple Springs building. Leaving the window slightly ajar, she stealthily kept watch and when the thieves arrived, she shot just above their heads to scare them off. They never returned!

In yet another case of larceny, Cecil felt as though her hands were tied. Some dishes and food had been stolen from her quarters, and shortly thereafter a family invited her to their home for dinner. When she sat down she recognized her own dishes and presumably her food there on the table. The people had stolen from her, and then invited her over to eat!

North Carolina or Tennessee?

The lumber mill company used to build chapels so that Cecil could minister to families while wood was being processed. Once the timber in a given area had been depleted, the company would move out and the need for the Army's religious services would end. The use of one particular chapel terminated prematurely, thanks to the state police. Although the chapel stood on the boundary between North Carolina and Tennessee, no one knew it when the building was constructed. But one day the police paid Cecil a visit.

"We can't do anything about the moonshiners up there because of your church," they informed her. "When we come to get them from North Carolina, they move to the side of the chapel that is in Tennessee. When the Tennessee boys come up here, the moonshiners go back over to the North Carolina side. So, Major, your church is going to have to go!"

Even though the chapel was torn down, Cecil continued to minister to the people in that area, using her jeep to reach them until the company moved out years later.

A Hostler's Curse

Aside from the moonshiners, Cecil also had to deal with a group of people known as "hostlers," itinerant backpackers who roamed the mountains with limited possessions. The mission reserved a small cabin for them where they could spend the night and eat a hot breakfast the next morning, all for one dollar.

Florence Wall remembers one hostler in his thirties who enjoyed spending time with the lieutenants. "He always wanted me to play the piano for him," she said. "He claimed to have a good baritone singing voice, and he wanted to practice – anything to get us girls together at the piano."

The presence of this young man displeased Cecil, who proceeded to run him off the mountain. Before he left, though, he pronounced doom on her and everything she did. The curse could have had lasting impact on the superstitious mountaineers, but, fortunately, it was soon forgotten, and life returned to normal.

Superstition wielded a major influence in the mountains during that era. One widespread belief was that placing an axe under the bed of a woman in labor would reduce her pain. Florence researched the subject of labor and childbirth and presented a program one Halloween called "A Feeling In Her Bones." Her listeners responded favorably because she tried to discredit mountain superstitions in a lighthearted way.

PROVIDING THE BASICS

The need to provide the basic necessities of life narrowed the gap between an insular culture and the outside world. Cecil made several visits to Asheville, often stopping at the big house behind the corps building where donated apparel was stored. She collected warm clothing, coats, blankets and other items, and she took them up the mountains to distribute to needy people. She also went to the area farmers' market, where friends would donate some of their food to the mission.

But communication remained quite limited because very few mountain families had telephones. The Salvation Army had one party line, so the women had to listen for their ring – two shorts and one long. Usually the caller would be someone who needed care for a sick family member or transportation to the hospital in Waynesville.

Most mountain people of Cecil's day have gone to Glory. The ones who remain were much younger than she was when the mission was in its heyday. There are still a few around, very old now themselves, but with vivid memories of what Cecil Brown meant to them and their families.

HELPING THE CAUSE

Troy Self, now in his eighties, considers Cecil Brown to be "the nearest thing to a celebrity" he ever knew. He praised her desire to serve the Lord under conditions that many people would consider next to impossible.

When Troy was 13 years old, he and his sisters began attending the Bonnie Hill Corps, just above where the family farm was located. By age 20, he used his truck to haul vegetables from the mission garden to the market, and to bring supplies up the mountain to corps stations, the school and the orphanage. He often drove to Hot Springs and other nearby communities to pick up people for special corps events such as a homecoming or a Singing Convention. Sometimes he took care of livery animals on the Army's farm. Although Cecil offered to pay him, he never accepted any money for his work.

"Cecil Brown was a wonderful woman of God," he said. "I think she lived what she taught. I went to one of her churches, and if she ever asked me to do something, I tried to do it for her. My family wasn't really in bad shape, so we didn't need the material assistance she often gave to others, but we needed her spiritual guidance and she was a good pastor to us. When my mother died, several of my sisters did go stay with her for awhile, and they helped in her work in very practical ways."

Troy saw many sides to Cecil, and he liked most of them. "I guess she did lose her temper on occasion, but you have to remember, she had a lot of things to worry about. She had a lot on her mind. A lot of people came to depend on her," he said.

The first associate officers' quarters

Chapter 13

The Heart of the Matter

Cecil Brown approached every facet of her work in a professional way. She always had a full schedule, and she focused intently on each individual task for the good of the whole ministry. In all aspects of her work, her main goal was to bring people to Christ.

Retired Major Glenna West said, "She concentrated on saving souls. That was her top priority. At one time she had seven churches and no assistant! But she did what we recommend today that missionaries do – train local people to take care of the program."

Cecil seemed happiest when she was with her people. When a writer from the *War Cry* asked to do a story on her, she shifted the spotlight to members of the corps.

"Major Brown did not make a big deal out of welfare programming," Glenna said. "She went to a home and if there was a need that she could supply, she did. She was interested in people, no matter who they were. She would sit by the bedside of a dying family member, and if she could do nothing but wash the person's face with a cold washcloth, she would do that. It seemed that no job was too menial for her."

"Many people found the Lord through the Army's work in the mountains because of Major Brown," Glenna said. "She was one of us. You knew it and you felt it. I gained so much in my one year with her before I went to training. It prepared me to serve the Lord as an officer. I've tried to follow the example she gave me."

PREACHING THE WORD

Cecil's style of preaching was anything but fiery. Actually, some people viewed Thelma Colton as a far better preacher. Cecil's message was plain – "If you don't come to the Lord, you are going to hell." Her sermons emphasized the love of God, and she had no tolerance for frivolity in her meetings.

Following in the footsteps of the master teacher, Cecil spread the gospel by meeting the practical needs of the people through a multitude of roles. Essentially, people recognized that although the road was a steady uphill grind, she never looked back – she always looked forward. Other people loved her, respected her ambitions, and gave her a helping hand. Sometimes, not enough, but she kept going. Her popularity resonated through a myriad of names that the people bestowed on her, including Maid of the Mountains, First Citizen of the Smokies, Shepherdess of the Hills, and God's Messenger on Horseback. The Army gave her the official title of District Officer of Mountain Missions.

No Nonsense

Dean Self remembers that Cecil approached her services in a very no-nonsense manner. She would reprimand anyone who even chuckled inappropriately while she was speaking. "I'm not going to put up with any laughing," she would warn.

Her impatience frequently rose to the surface when she was interrupted. Once a lady held a child who was crying and screaming during a service. Cecil was trying to preach and the lady just sat there while the baby disrupted the service. Finally, unable to bear the noise any longer, Cecil stopped in mid-sentence and exclaimed, "Lady, please take that child out of here!"

Some mountain people believed that if God spoke to them, they should stand up and share their divine encounter with the congregation. "One old man got up and told his testimony and went on and on, right in the middle of Major Brown's altar invitation," Dean said. "Major said, 'Let's have a little more praying, and less talking, please!'"

During one service held at Big Bend, the song leader was leading the music with whatever songs came to mind. "Soon, Aunt Cecil got up and said, 'Well, that's fine, but now let's sing some religious songs so we can go on with our service,'" her niece, June Brown, said.

"She loved all gospel songs," June said, "but especially the lively ones. And she could play all of them on her harp. She had a lovely soprano singing voice. Just after I got married, she returned from a conference in Atlanta and brought me an accordion. I was so surprised and thrilled, and I played it for her services for a long time."

Wayne Moore appreciated her preaching style because she spoke in a way that mountain people could understand. "She always talked about the Lord, and how He would save us if only we repented of our sins. She constantly taught that He was willing to save us," he said. Cecil's own assessment was that "the mountain people are not easy to win for Christ, but they stick when they are won."

Wayne worked in the family business of moonshining, although that never became an issue with Cecil. "There were moonshiners all around here," he said. "She was on a crusade against white liquor, and she tried to get the moonshiners to stop. She did her best to talk them out of making it. But we knew she cared about us, and she only wanted to get us saved and into church."

A PERSONAL TOUCH

"Cecil Brown was a unique person," Wayne said. "She was always the same whenever you saw her. It didn't take her long to get to know you and to remember your name. She knew just how to talk to you and get you interested in what she was saying. She won many people in the mountains to Christ."

Dorothy Langston echoed Wayne's sentiments. "She knew the names of all the families and all the children."

Blanche Lowe saw the secret of Cecil's success in the way she related to the moonshiners. She said that Cecil could have met opposition from people who had stills hidden on their property if she had turned them in. Instead, she let them know that she thought moonshining was a sin, but she never reported them, and that made them trust her all the more. Later on, when she preached to these same people, they would listen and their hearts would be touched.

"If they hadn't trusted her, she wouldn't have been able to accomplish all that she did. Mountain people were different then. Back then, if you were from 'the outside' (down the mountains) you were not trusted," Blanche said.

Trophies of Grace

One particular moonshiner, who was gloriously saved, numbers among Cecil's greatest trophies. Cecil visited him a couple of times each week that first month, because, as she put it, "he has his own still and the temptation to backslide is great." On one visit, the man invited Cecil to watch him empty all his liquor onto the ground, and then break up his still with an axe. He joined a corps and held several local lay leadership positions.

Fanny Rathbone's family started attending Army services at the first established mission. The Rathbones came solely because Cecil went out of her way to visit them. "I had six brothers and sisters – so the seven of us kids went, as well as my mother and father," Fanny said.

Fanny spoke of Cecil's visits to her home. "We would sit and talk for hours about the Bible. She loved to talk about the Lord to me." Fanny particularly enjoyed special meetings that took place at the Maple Springs Corps. "Sometimes that church was so full you couldn't get anyone else inside. There'd be people outside listening through the windows. Sometimes she would play her harp and concertina and lead us in singing. If you named a gospel song, she probably knew it, and we'd sing it. She knew just about all the old songs."

Cecil assigned a mission post to each one of her assistants. They would plan a Vacation Bible School, gather a week's supply of food and materials, and pick up as many as 20 children on their way to the mission station. On one trip, they gave rides to three brothers named Matthew, Mark and Luke (there was no John). During the day the children learned Bible verses, sang choruses, played and made a craft. At the end of the day, the teachers would walk the children home.

Lumber Camps

Thelma Hall grew up in a lumber mill family that Cecil ministered to as part of an arrangement she had with the company's owner, Harry Liner. Thelma said, "It's hard to express how I feel about Cecil Brown because I was young when I first met The Salvation Army, and I was attracted to the Army uniform. I was completely taken in by the services and immediately attracted to Cecil Brown's leadership."

A group of young people, including Thelma, made circuit rounds with Cecil to conduct meetings at Bonnie Hill, Shelton Laurel, Cold Creek and Spring Creek. In each of the corps, she recalled, many people attended the meetings faithfully and seemed to eagerly anticipate coming to worship the Lord.

One service in particular led to a noteworthy conversion, according to Thelma. "My father's boss, Mr. Liner, came to one of the meetings in the chapel that his lumber company built for us. We all knew that Mr. Liner had a drinking problem. On this Sunday night, I went up to him and spoke to him about his soul. He gave his heart to the Lord! He lived a fine Christian life thereafter, and the community knew how wonderful he was."

Thelma left the mountains to follow her own calling. She saw Cecil again a few more times, including on her wedding day in 1944. Her love and respect for Major Brown never diminished – in fact, she considers Cecil one of the blessings that helped her through the difficulties in her life.

Cecil set up a partnership with Boyce Hardwood Company to build the corps at Cold Springs. It was an oral contract based on mutual trust that could not be reached as easily today, if at all. She went directly to Colonel Boyce and told him exactly what she needed. "I'd like to have some lumber to build my churches," she said. They shook hands and he replied, "Okay – I'll build a church for you if you stay down here and preach. These people need it." The community of Cold Springs then consisted of 50 unchurched families.

True to his word, Mr. Boyce built the chapel and put a sign above the front door: "Cecil/Thelma Chapel," named for Cecil Brown and Thelma Colton. They conducted corps meetings there for many years, until Boyce Hardwood went out of business and the community dried up.

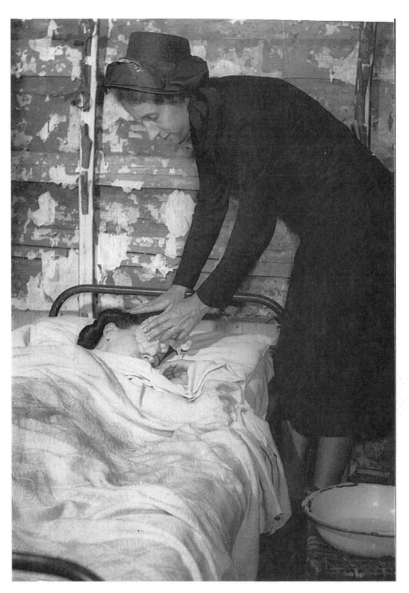

Major Brown soothes a fevered brow.

Chapter 14

Inside the Mission

To meet her financial obligations, and more importantly, to prove to Salvation Army stalwarts that their gamble in sending her to the mountains had succeeded, Cecil initiated several commercial ventures within the ministry.

First, she opened a trading post that sold a variety of items to both local residents and visiting tourists. The store sat across the road from the Maple Springs Citadel, where mountain women could learn how to weave and practice their craft. They wove rugs, tea towels, scarves, bedspreads and quilts, and then they sold their wares to help finance the work of the Army.

While money remained scarce, the mountaineers used a bartering system to share needed goods. A dozen eggs would buy a pound of coffee. Gasoline was sold from a pump located onsite.

Cecil also recruited itinerant migrant workers to help harvest the crops. The mission had a contract with the Stokeley Foods Company to can vegetables that were grown at Maple Springs. Everyone worked in the fields, including Major Brown and her lieutenants, and they had a garden that provided fruits and vegetables.

STRAWBERRY JAM

When berry-picking season arrived, Cecil wanted to can enough berries for at least 100 jars of strawberry and huckleberry jams. The women brought with them everything they needed for canning – jars, buckets, sugar and other supplies. Each person would sit in one place and pick a bucket of berries, capping them one by one. The group also canned meats such as hog meat, sausage and hams to eat throughout the winter and to sell at the trading post. Vegetables, including cabbage, turnips and greens, were preserved and stored underground.

One night Doris McQuay and Marjorie Key had been picking greens for supper when a carload of Salvation Army officers pulled up. Someone in the car called out, "Are you coming to Junaluska for Officers' Councils tomorrow?" Doris shouted back, "When we get our work done here, we will." Her answer brought an appreciative smile to Cecil's face.

TAMBOURINES

Saturday collection routes usually offered a reliable source of donations for Salvation Army ministries. With tambourines and an ample supply of *War Crys* in hand, Cecil and her assistants would travel from town to town following carefully planned agendas. Invariably, they dressed in full uniform with bonnets, wearing black hose with perfectly straight seams.

Their routes carried them as far away as Murphy, N.C., and into northern Georgia. Sometimes the women would pile into a motel room and then follow another course back the next day. Often money was hard to come by – one diary entry noted that Cecil drove 177 miles to collect just ten dollars. Another read, "Evelyn and I collected in Sylva, Franklin, and along the highway to Asheville. The collection was not so very good. But I won't complain."

Florence Wall recounted stopping at a courthouse where "a bunch of old mountain men were just sitting around as though they were waiting for something to happen." Holding her tambourine in one hand, she began to climb the courthouse steps. One of the old men yelled, "Sister!"

Florence didn't know he was talking to her, so she kept on walking. He hollered louder, "Sister – I'm talking to you!"

"What is it, sir?"

"I want to ask you something. Do you beg all the time?"

"No sir. I don't beg all the time – just on Saturdays." The old men all laughed hard, and he spit out a wad of tobacco juice and said, "That's all, Sister – you can go now!"

Dean Self told the story of a collection day in downtown Waynesville when a crowd had gathered along the sidewalk. As Cecil neared the horde of people, she found them huddled around a small man who was being beaten up. She started to break up the crowd and pull the aggressor off this poor fellow. Just then a woman stopped her and said, "Major, that's my husband getting a whoppin', and he deserves it!"

Another time a man walked up to Cecil, dropped a nickel into the tambourine, and asked the major to pray for rain. Cecil was not the least bit impressed. "I don't think the Lord sends five-cent rains," she said.

Doris McQuay recalled with pathos the dire poverty of the Cherokee Indians in North Carolina. Many native Americans would put a buffalo nickel in her tambourine, she said, which for them was as generous as the meager donation made by the poor widow in the New Testament.

"Everyone in those little towns knew Cecil and loved her. All she had to do was walk down the street and people would come to her with their money. We got to one town that was really nothing more than just a wide spot in the road. She said to me, 'You sit in the jeep and I'll collect this whole town.'

"I said, 'Major, I don't feel comfortable doing that – I'll do one side and you do the other.' But she said, 'No – I have to go down and come back anyway, so I'll do both sides of the street.'"

Doris kept an eye on Cecil's bonnet as she made her way to the far end of the street, and then back up. That day, she realized that Cecil never asked anyone to do anything that she would not do herself, and she began to truly appreciate her mentor's unfailing dedication to the cause.

On one trip the two women had finished collecting on their routes and were heading back up the mountains. About halfway home, it started to snow, and the higher and higher they climbed, the harder it seemed to snow. Finally the jeep couldn't go any further. Cecil told Doris, "I'm going for help. You stay here."

To the Rescue!

This time Doris insisted on joining her, so off they went up the snowy mountain road. Before long they met Mr. Presnell, one of their recruits, coming down the mountain with his horse. He had known it was time for them to arrive, and he also realized that they would never make it up that mountain road in the jeep. So he quickly hitched up the horse to the jeep and towed it home to Maple Springs. "Major Brown and I walked because we both felt sorry for the horse," Doris said. "When we got home, we thawed out by the fire, and we were fine."

Hospital Visits

For Mildred Kirby, interpersonal relationships meant as much or more than collecting dollars and cents for the Salvation Army. As part of her League of Mercy work, she had to walk through the hospital hallways distributing the *War Cry*, although she could not accept donations. One ward held six beds and a single patient who lay sound asleep. As Mildred prepared to leave, she heard him say, "Hey, Sallie! Don't leave."

She turned around to face him and he said, "I want you to pray for me."

"I was scared to death!" she recalls now. "But I did it. I went back and prayed for him."

Cecil Brown, M.D.

Cecil served as a surrogate country doctor for many families in the mountains. She gave needed medical assistance to the locals on countless occasions. Once she was hoeing in her garden at Maple Springs and heard someone wailing down in the valley below. She rushed out and about a mile away she found a young man crawling along a mountain trail, bleeding heavily. He had shot himself in the leg. Cecil quickly applied a tourniquet and saved his life. Another time she was called to a cabin four miles away to help an elderly woman who had fallen into an open fireplace. Cecil was able to relieve her burns and prevent a dangerous infection.

She made use of home remedies, including a root that when mixed with "a wee-bit of white lightning" was believed to cure a variety of ills. One afternoon, while June and Reese Ferguson were on a trip into town, she was babysitting their daughter Nancy, who was two years old. When they returned, Cecil told June that she had "doctored" Nancy while they were gone.

"How did you doctor her?" June asked.

"She just needed a tonic," Cecil said.

Making a tea out of wild herbs, she had given it to Nancy to drink. A little later, after Cecil had left, Nancy broke out in a rash. "But that's the kind of doctoring that older people practiced in those days," June said.

The people of Cecil's generation believed firmly in the value of cod liver oil. "Aunt Cecil thought that every spring you had to have your blood purified," June said. "So she would go to the drug store in town and buy something called 'Sulfur Wafers.' You took one of those with a good dose of cod-liver oil and that purified your blood – if you could stand it!"

"She was a nurse, doctor, teacher – whatever was needed," said Glenna West, who benefited from many of these services. "I suspect that the time I spent in the mountains with her made me conscious of the importance of loving people. That if I couldn't help make a difference in their lives, then I was a failure. All the bricks and mortar we put together means very little."

Fanny Rathbone often accompanied Cecil on her rounds to care for the sick. "I loved to go with her to doctor people," Fanny said. "Sometimes the call came in the middle of the night, and if I was around she took me, too. Anywhere there was someone who needed her help, there she'd go.

"My husband, Lloyd, was very sick at one point. She would come up here and give him medicine – sometimes injections – until she could do no more."

Blanche Lowe also assisted in Cecil's medical ministry. "She never stopped, no matter how cold it was or how bad the roads were – if there was a need, even in the middle of the night if someone came knocking on the door, or if someone needed a doctor or a ride to the hospital she'd take them," Blanche said. "I don't know what many of the mountain people would have done without her. I know that some of them would have died if Cecil Brown had not been there for them. The days were never too bad or the nights too dark for her to lend a helping hand."

In one of her reports, the beloved "Maid of the Mountains" wrote: "My first-aid training is standing me in good stead and it is constantly in demand. The mountain people depend on me to get them to the hospital."

Fortunately, Cecil knew when her limited medical expertise should give way to a professionally trained physician. Jean Frese recalls the time when a person had to be taken to the hospital, and the snow was so deep that the jeep could not go up or down the mountain. Cecil simply hitched up a sled to her horse, put the sick person on the sled, and rode to town.

"She had no formal medical training, but she trained herself and she trained me too," Jean said. Cecil even taught Jean how to give injections.

"She showed me how to give a shot to someone, and said that she would give me an orange to practice on. But then something came up, and she had to send me to one sick man who needed a shot, and I had to give it to him without any practice! It obviously went okay, because he didn't die."

HOME SCHOOL

The school at the Mountain Mission played a primary role in Cecil's ministry. The geographic isolation of the children made their education extremely difficult, if not impossible. The school also ran an orphanage for children who had lost either one or both parents. On one occasion a widower brought his child to the mission because he had to work and could not take care of her anymore.

Cecil took on the role of the children's legal guardian and supervised their housing and education. They lived at Maple Springs, and The Salvation Army became their home. Florence Wall, who had a teacher's certificate and credentials from Centenary College, taught the first three grades during the time she worked with Cecil. She remembers one 15-year old boy who had never learned to read. Florence taught him the alphabet and later he learned how to read and write. The children affectionately dubbed their school "Possum College."

According to Wayne Moore, "She took in and kept a lot of children, and the Lord only knows what would have happened to them if it weren't for Cecil Brown. Most of them didn't have a family and had nowhere else to go."

"When my mother passed away, I was nine," June Brown said. "There were other children living with her, and I was one of the youngest. Every child had special chores to do, such as laundry, milking cows and churning butter. Blanche and I cooked. We had to gather firewood. Our only running water was across the road and behind our trading post. And the only way to fill the water tank was by pumping it. So if you happened to leave the water running and it dried up, you were expected to go and hand-pump that thing until the tank filled back up!"

By the time electricity came into use, June was in the tenth grade. After she reached adulthood and married, many more children came to live with Cecil at the home. One family of brothers and sisters arrived, and the youngest of them was a toddler.

Blanche Lowe came to live with Cecil because she had an illness resembling asthma, and she could not walk the distance from her home to the school. She remembers one family with five children whose heartbroken father brought them to the mission to live after their mother had left the family.

Cecil kept a little paddle called the "Token of Love" to deter any misbehavior. Blanche recalls a few straps of leather on the paddle, making it look all the more ominous. "She never used it on us, of course. It just hung somewhere on the wall so we could see it, and we all stayed in line without her ever having to use it that I can remember."

After Florence Wall married, she and her husband Jack were working for the Army in Niagara Falls, New York. Florence opened a Christmas letter from one of her students, Lela Presnell, who wrote: "I hope you remember me. I saw your picture in the *War Cry* and I wanted you to know how much it meant for me to get an education, and that you made me hunger for a higher education. After you left the mountains I went on to college with some financial help from my uncle, and now I am teaching Spanish in New Jersey. I even married Mickey Brown (another of the students from the Army's school at Maple Springs)."

MRS. CLAUS

Each year Christmas in the mountains held special meaning for Cecil. Her family had been too poor to afford presents, and she wanted the children to enjoy what she had missed. Since many mountain families lacked trees and decorations, they would celebrate Christmas at their corps. "I know of one family who got a doll for their little girl, and she had only certain hours in any given day when she could take that doll down to play with it – and then only under adult supervision!" Jean Frese said.

Cecil made sure that every corps had a Christmas party, and she encouraged the people to exchange their gifts at the party. In an upstairs room at the trading post, known as the "Christmas Room," she kept reserves of toys and supplies. One year Glenna West noticed that her hands were scratched, cut, and bleeding from wrapping so many gifts. She offered to help, but Cecil refused, saying, "No, wrapping these gifts is part of my gift to these people." Men usually received handkerchiefs and ties, while women unwrapped various presents such as handbags, aprons, and kitchen items. The children, of course, were always thrilled with an assortment of different toys.

Cecil and her assistants would perform a new play every year, which was staged at each of the mission corps. One comedy, called "Christmas at the Poor Farm," featured Cecil and her sisters playing four old ladies who lived in a poor house. It was a huge hit!

Dean Self smiled broadly as she described the Christmas plays and parties at her Bonnie Hill Corps. Dean's mother had died when she was only two years old, and her father moved the family there from Wolf Creek, Tennessee. They took a short walk down the mountain to Bonnie Hill, and since her father was a religious man, the family attended services regularly. The corps became the center of Dean's life.

"One Christmas, Major Brown bought me a dress, and I was so excited over having something pretty to wear! She had tons of stuff because a lot of merchants were happy to help her with her work. After our Christmas dramas, we would distribute gifts. I remember one year she gave every family a fruitcake. Well, up in the mountains a fruitcake was made with applesauce – it wasn't at all like the fruitcakes we know about, and a lot of the mountain folks really didn't care for the fruitcakes from the city!"

The Bonnie Hill Corps relied on Florence Wall to play the part of Santa Claus. "I had the pillows, the red suit, the beard – everything," she said. "I wanted to surprise the people in the chapel, so I had to be pushed through a small window in the back room, and enter the chapel from that angle. Unfortunately, I got stuck in the window! I couldn't go forwards or backwards. They had a ball with me. They left me stranded there, halfway in and halfway out. The corps people thought that was the funniest thing they had ever seen. I understand they talked about that night for many Christmases long after I left."

Singing Convention

High on the list of Cecil's priorities was the annual Singing Convention. Musicians would travel from miles around to perform at this popular event, and hundreds of gospel music lovers attended just to enjoy the merriment. In the early years polio epidemics and heavy rains affected the size of the crowds. But even with these major obstacles, people seemed to come from everywhere – in cars, trucks, wagons, on horseback, and even on foot. One year, more than 2,000 delegates represented ten different states.

A 1949 *War Cry* article described a surprisingly eclectic class of people on hand for this popular event:

> So who attends these singing conventions, one might ask. To find his answer, he has only to look about him at the stream of humanity dressed in its Sunday best, which emerges from snug little mountain cabins hugged close to green hillsides . . . from the small neighboring communities . . . from a lumber camp here and an imposing farmhouse there . . . or perhaps from an Indian reservation in the national forest area. These people are the real mountaineers, not only the rustics who have never so much as strayed from their own cornfield, but men and women and young folks who have attended the city schools and so-journed in urban communities. Many of these people have traveled abroad, only to find that the world has nothing better to offer them than the security of a farm and the privilege of working one's land and rearing one's family away from the confusion of the big city.

Cecil and her assistants sold fried chicken dinners to those who arrived without their own lunches, which created an annual boon for the mission's financial ledger. According to Doris McQuay, the home-cooked feast embodied a true labor of love. She and her close friend, Captain Nelda Stephenson, killed the chickens together. "Nelda and I helped pluck feathers off those dead chickens, and I've never seen that many feathers before or since!"

June Brown also witnessed many years of killing, plucking and frying chickens. Her father and her uncle would fry chickens all night long before the convention. "It was a lot of work, but it was important to Aunt Cecil because of her dedication and her love for her people. You just don't see that level of caring anymore," June said. "If there is any doubt as to why she was successful– that's why."

Spreading the joy of Christmas

Chapter 15

Working with Cecil

Cecil Brown's loyal supporters saw her as a modern-day apostle who could do no wrong. They described her as loving, compassionate and tireless in her efforts to help the needy. Yet outspoken critics – usually people from outside of the mountains – called her unfeeling, stubborn, vengeful, and downright vain. In their minds, though Cecil may have been divinely chosen at the right time and for the right situation – she could *do* few things right. Her detractors argued that those who put her on a pedestal did not have to work with her. Others simply recognized her as a multi-faceted human being who had both strengths and growing edges. Some admirers admitted that she was obstinate and even high-strung. And even the most vocal opponents were willing to concede that her efficiency and her puritan work ethic offered a role model for others.

"Though she received the Order of the Founder, the first one for the Southern Territory, I can't say I ever saw her wearing that badge," Glenna West said. "She never brought it out. I think that any honor The Salvation Army could give to her never meant a thing to her because it didn't mean anything to her people. What mattered to the people is what mattered to her."

Few would deny that she loved the Lord and her people. Everything she did was for Him and for them. Cecil was a missionary in the truest sense. Given the economic, cultural and geographical climate of western North Carolina, her mission could just as easily have taken place on a desert island or in an undeveloped part of Africa.

The Mountain Way

When Cecil left home in the mid-1920s she entered a vastly different world from the one she had known before. Her exposure to modern life made her yearn to help the folks she had left behind. While not compromising their uniqueness, she wanted a better life for them than they knew. First and foremost, they needed the gospel. But she also wanted desperately to uplift them by means of physical, social and economic assistance. For these reasons, the mountaineers understood her and she understood them. Years before the mission got its name, the locals simply called it "Cecil Brown's work." Mountaineers continually fought to survive, and they had no frame of reference apart from their hardscrabble existence. If the work of the Salvation Army was to succeed, it had to be done on their terms.

Her personality reflected the unique culture in which she grew up. Mountain people have always had good hearts. They would share freely whatever was growing in their garden with a visitor. If they killed a hog, they would give a visitor some meat to take home to cook. When anyone in the community got sick, neighbors would sit up all night with that person or tend to their fields. A friend in the mountains always proved faithful. Under the direction of Cecil Brown, the Army's ministry was a microcosm of a culture that was caring and altruistic.

Cecil gave no compliments, measured her words, showed a hint of drollness, and maintained a work ethic that demanded as much of her as it did of others. She shared an emotional reserve with many of her family, friends and hundreds of others who flocked to her mission stations. "The nearest thing to a compliment she gave me," said one lieutenant, "came when I preached for about 25 minutes at the corps in Timber Ridge (Tennessee), and after I finished she got up and told the congregation, 'This lady can say more in five minutes than I can in 30 – we have time for some testimonies!'"

Army Protocol

According to Thelma Hall, Cecil's staff greatly anticipated their occasional trips to Atlanta. "Usually Major Brown would take three or four young people with her and we couldn't wait to go to Atlanta to witness the commissioning, as well as to the Trade Department where we got new uniforms and bonnets," she said. "Everything had to be perfect as far as Major Brown was concerned. She was a perfectionist, and many people didn't like her for that very reason – but I liked it. Her sternness was good for us, and it helped me through the years to do things the right way."

The seams on the women's hose had to line up perfectly straight. The hems of their skirts had to be 12 inches from the floor. Their hair had to be in a perfect bun. No jewelry was allowed. "We knew we were different, but it didn't seem to make any difference to us. We enjoyed it," she said.

Cecil almost always traveled in uniform, probably more for protection than out of allegiance to Army regulations. A pitchfork or a rifle could easily greet any strange visitor to a mountain homestead, so recognition was important. "When she approached our house, even from far down the trail we could spot her bonnet and we knew who it was," one mountain resident said.

A former assistant explained, "Most of the lieutenants who came to help her were 'from down below the ridge'— that was the expression mountain people used to describe anyone from civilization." So it was important for them to wear the uniform.

An Officer Trio

In what may have been an unprecedented commissioning, Lieutenants Mildred Kirby, Mildred Gentry and Florence Wall – all members of the Warriors Session – received their first appointment in 1947 to the mountains. Arriving after midnight and excited about working in this legendary ministry, they marveled at the beauty of the moonlight on the mountain roads.

"My first impression of Cecil Brown was that she was all business," Florence said. "She usually thought a lot before she proceeded with anything. I realized she was the leader and she made sure everyone else realized that, too. I learned quite a bit from her."

Cecil drove the lieutenants hard. Today very few new captains would do the menial tasks these city girls did in their first appointment as Salvation Army officers. They wallpapered and painted their own housing quarters, affectionately known as "the birdhouse." In addition to running the corps mission stations, they tended their own gardens and raised their own food. A few months after the trio arrived at the mission, the divisional commander, Colonel Gus Stephans, paid a visit. He found it hard to believe that the young women did all the things he had heard about. He'd say, "Why do you do all that? That's not what you were sent up here for!"

Mildred Kirby, who was perhaps the most outspoken of the three lieutenants, answered, "Don't tell us; tell her! We do what we are told to do. When we get up in the morning and she tells us to go pick beans in the field, what are we supposed to say? You just can't tell Cecil Brown, 'That's not what I was sent here for!'"

A few years after Mildred was transferred from her post, Colonel Stephans asked her again, "Tell me the truth. Did you really pick beans in the field?"

"Yes, and I've got pictures to prove it. Cecil Brown ran that mission like a little platoon. She loved the structure and the order of things. She made menus and lined up the chores and the work assignments for each week."

The title of one of Cecil's books, *Long-Haired Bossy Wives and Women Preachers*, by Dr. John R. Rice, happened to catch Mildred's attention. He was a holiness preacher from Tennessee who opposed the role of women in ministry. Mildred asked to read it, but Cecil would not loan it to her. She decided to "borrow" the book anyway and then she returned it without Cecil's knowledge!

Mildred enjoyed her work at the corps, even though it was arduous, and she reminisced fondly about her days as an officer. "I remember once when Cecil asked us to take some of the children into town. Can you imagine being eight or nine years old and never having been to a town? We drove the jeep to Waynesville, about 25 miles from Maple Springs. Zeta Fleming, Florence Wall and I had about ten kids with us. These kids were bug-eyed – they just wanted to see everything all at once! We were laughing at them, because they were so excited. Cecil had given them a little money, and we took them to the five-and-dime store. They were overwhelmed because it was the first real store they had ever been in!"

CONFRONTATION

If Mildred Kirby was the most outspoken in a long line of Cecil's assistants, Florence Wall held her tongue more than the others – until one day when her frustrations reached a boiling point. Cecil had blamed her lieutenants for something that her mother had done, but Florence didn't want to make an issue of it. She finally surprised Cecil by standing her ground. "Major, I've always respected you and your authority here, but in this case I think you're wrong. You're coming down too hard on the lieutenants and I am one of them. I don't appreciate it and I'm not going to put up with it any longer. We all feel the same way I do, but the others are afraid of you – I'm not!"

At first Cecil was taken aback. After a few moments she managed to respond, "How dare you talk to me like that!"

Florence shot back, "Yes, I *do* dare. And I don't feel good about it." For a while, Cecil eased up on the lieutenants, and the near-mutiny subsided.

Despite her tense altercation with Cecil, Florence found great pleasure in her work in the mountains. "When I left there, one of the older women made me a quilt. She said, 'You are the quietest lieutenant! It was hard getting to know you because you're so quiet. But my family wants you to have this quilt so you won't ever forget us.' And I never have. They were wonderful people. I think I became one of them and they took me in," she said.

By the time she received orders for her next appointment, Florence was engaged to Lieutenant Jack Brewer. Although Cecil hated to see her go, she wished her Godspeed, and she sent her a salary check that had been delayed due to a shortage of funds. Florence sent back a tithe in her thank-you card, which was unexpected, and Cecil wrote back expressing her appreciation.

Glenna West had been picking beans on the family farm near Little Creek Corps when Cecil tried to recruit her to work in the mountains. Since she planned to be an Army officer, she had decided to work with Cecil before entering the training college. "The first thing Major Brown had me do as her assistant was to go out in the Army's patch and pick beans! I remember thinking that I really hadn't come all that far yet!"

About a year later, when the time came for Glenna to leave, Cecil tried to dissuade her on their way to Atlanta. Every few miles she'd turn to me and say, "Are you sure you want to do this? Because I could teach you everything you need to know about working with people." Cecil knew a good thing when she had it, and she did not want to let her go. Glenna eventually returned to the mountains as an officer to command her home corps of Little Creek, which included her own family as parishioners. Altogether, she spent a total of five years working with Cecil in a unique and rewarding role.

Zeta Fleming, Cecil and Florence Wall visit the city.

Chapter 16

The Rules of the Road

As more women lieutenants came to work at the mission, Cecil gained a reputation as a harsh taskmaster. Doris McQuay remembers an incident that embarrassed her greatly at the time. On her commissioning Sunday, she received orders to go the Mountain Mission, and she had an opportunity to introduce her mother to Cecil. Mrs. McQuay, who was concerned about her daughter's future, pleaded, "Major Brown, please don't work my daughter too hard in the fields – she has bad feet and legs!"

"If the floor had opened up," Doris said, "I would have jumped down into it, I was so embarrassed." The expression on Cecil's face was priceless. Unamused, she calmly informed Mrs. McQuay, "I don't <u>make</u> my people do those things."

On the way from Atlanta to the mountains, Doris asked Cecil how long the trip would take. "About eight hours," Cecil said, "but it only takes seven hours to drive from there to Atlanta." When a bewildered Doris questioned the obvious discrepancy, Cecil explained with a smile that it was all uphill to the mountains, and all downhill to Atlanta.

Many of the traditional mountain customs puzzled Doris, who had grown up in the city of Baltimore. She learned, for instance, that if a woman passed a strange man while driving down a mountain road and he waved to her, she should ignore him.

"I don't understand all this – I thought we are supposed to be friendly," Doris said. Cecil said, "Not unless you know them. If you know them, you can wave at them, but only if they wave first!"

HANGING LINGERIE

One of Doris' most comical lessons stemmed from something as innocent as hanging out the wash to dry. She had hung her laundry on the clothesline behind the house where she and Lieutenant Marjorie Key were living. Later that day Cecil walked over to the building where the dining room was located, and she turned to Doris and Marjorie. "Whose laundry is that on the clothesline?" she asked.

Doris smiled and said, "That's mine."

Cecil was incredulous. "You can't hang your laundry like that here in the mountains!"

Doris didn't back down. "Well, that's the way my mother taught me to hang laundry – all my slips together, all my blouses together, all my panties and bras together, and so on."

"Well," Cecil said, "You can't do that up here. You have to hang your underwear behind your other clothes, so people coming up the road won't see it."

Doris fired back: "_What people_ coming up the road? We're a hundred miles from nowhere!"

Cooling down a bit, Cecil explained, "Haven't you seen logging trucks coming up the road? If the truckers see lingerie hanging on a clothesline, that's an invitation to them to stop in!" It didn't take long for Doris to rearrange her clothes, and from then on she never relayed the inadvertently amorous signal again.

COMING WITH DOUBTS

Perhaps Jean Frese retained more from her experiences than anyone else who assisted Cecil. Although she felt strongly about accepting Cecil's invitation to join her, upon her arrival she struggled with ambivalence. In Waynesville, she decided to check into an old hotel across from the train station, take a shower and rest before she went up into the mountains.

"For a little while there, I thought I had made a big mistake in agreeing to come," Jean said. "I went down to the drug store, and one of the ladies behind the counter just smiled at me. I later learned that she was a wonderful Christian. But it was her smile that encouraged me so I decided to give this a try. I'm so glad I did."

Eyeopeners

If there are friendly people like her, thought Jean, *then this is the place the Lord wants me to be.* Then someone from the mission arrived to drive her up the mountain. She watched the paved road turn into a dirt road, and then the dirt road ended! She found a life where there were no telephones and where the people cooked on woodstoves. She thought, *Oh no!* But she stayed anyway.

Her memories are ones of great fulfillment. "On my first day with Cecil, she tried to break me in real well," Jean said. "Someone was killing a hog, and she took me to see it. She was watching my reaction. While they were getting ready to kill this hog, we saw two ladies across from us who put two of their fingers up to their mouths and spit out tobacco juice. I was watching them and I guess my eyes were as big as saucers. And Cecil was getting a real kick out of watching my reaction. I looked over at her and her eyes were just twinkling. That tickled her to death."

The next day, while visiting Poplar Gap, Cecil and Jean sat next to a woman who was nursing her baby. Apparently Cecil guessed that Jean had never seen anything like that before. Again, Jean noticed Cecil's eyes dancing. She didn't really crack a smile, but her eyes said it all. Another time they went to visit a woman who was in dire need of the Army's help. They crossed over an old bridge near her house, and Jean saw some pigs in the yard below. As they grew closer the woman came out, and Cecil spoke first: "We hear that you folks need a little help."

"People know more about our business than we do!" the old mountain woman shouted back.

"Now just calm down and sit here for a minute and we'll talk," Cecil said calmly. "Jean, you sit here on this chair."

The chair had no support, and as Jean sat down, she leaned back and tumbled over onto the floor. Both Cecil and the old mountain woman roared. "Well, at least she's getting broken in!" Cecil said. Jean's mishap put the elderly woman at ease, and she gratefully accepted the Army's offer of food and clothes for her family.

Mountain Citizenship

Jean literally had to learn the ropes. During her first couple of weeks, she and Cecil followed a trail leading to Newport in Madison County where several families were visited regularly. To Jean's dismay, the pair had to swing Tarzan-style across a ravine! But as soon as the government cleared the way for Interstate 40, the need for rope swinging came to an end.

Her lessons in mountain life continued to unfold. One Sunday School class, which was held high up on one of the mountains, could only be reached by horseback. While Ernest Presnell saddled the horse for her, she mentioned her plans to visit a family along the way. Mr. Presnell began stroking his chin and mused, "If you were my young'un – I wouldn't let you go."

"Why, Ernest, what's the trouble?"

"Well, I heard that the wife is away for a few days, and if the wife is not there, it isn't fittin' that you go."

Jean took Ernest's advice and mentally filed away another unwritten mountain rule.

Jean struggled long and hard for acceptance from the mountain people, and an act of loving kindness sealed her attachment to them for the rest of her life. Her two hardest adjustments included food and mountain "language." In fact, she had so much trouble adjusting to the food that she dropped from 155 to 88 pounds. She would often ask Cecil, "When am I going to belong with the mountain folk?"

Finally the day arrived when Cecil handed Jean an official "mountain citizenship paper." In Cecil's own handwriting, it read: "To be a mountaineer: talk our language, eat our food, and become one of us in every way." Cecil had signed it, whole-heartedly assuring her that she qualified as a mountain citizen in every way. "So from then on I was a mountaineer!" Jean beamed.

NO FEAR

Jean marveled at Cecil's composure in the face of danger. She recalled a domestic crisis involving a man who had threatened to shoot his entire family with a rifle. One of the man's sons sneaked away, ran the three miles to Maple Springs, and alerted Cecil. She quickly jumped in her jeep, drove to the site and said calmly, "All right, give me the gun."

"He just handed it over to her," Jean said.

One day Jean, Blanche Lowe and other assistants journeyed to collect money for the Army, leaving Cecil behind at Maple Springs. The weather had turned bad, and snow and ice made driving difficult. At one perilous bend in the road, the jeep skidded and dangled precariously on the edge of a cliff. Afraid to go any further, they summoned Cecil for help. When she arrived, she jumped into the jeep and drove it safely forward. The group, non-plussed, stared in amazement as she called out to them, "Well, what are you waiting for? Get in!"

On yet another trip, Cecil had been traveling alone and failed to return home on time. Several young women hiked down the road to look for her, finding her empty car in a ravine, with Cecil nowhere in sight. They later learned that the car had left the road, rolled over, and rested on its wheels with her still inside. Miraculously, she had been unharmed. She simply climbed out of the ravine and walked back to town to find someone who would tow the car back to mission headquarters.

"A lot of people thought she was not an easy person to get along with," Blanche Lowe said. "I didn't see it that way. She had a mission in life and she did it. It might have shortened her life, because she didn't get enough rest, and she exposed herself to the cold. When you ride a horse in zero-degree weather to hold church services, or to see about someone who is sick at all hours of the night and in every kind of weather – that takes a toll on you."

"Major Brown had a temper, but she never yelled at us," Thelma Hall said. "She just expected us to do our work and to do our best at it. If we didn't, we'd hear about it."

THE WAY IT WAS

Thelma described as "tender" an incident that exemplified three of Cecil's strongest traits: sternness, patience, and a low-key sense of humor: Once while leading a youth program, Thelma began reading aloud the poem *Trees* by Joyce Kilmer. She got tickled and by the end of the poem, she was in "a downright laughing mode." She looked up and Cecil said, "Thelma, I think it's time you go into the back room of the chapel and stay there until you settle down!" After Thelma finally composed herself, she returned to the chapel and Cecil allowed her to proceed with the program.

"I've heard that many people think she was hard to get along with," Glenna West said. " I don't recall it that way, except for one time when she came down hard on me for something, then when she realized she was wrong she came to me and apologized."

"She always treated you fairly, no matter what," Jean Frese said. "It may not have seemed so at the time. Some of the girls didn't like to be around her because they didn't understand her. But she really was protecting them because of the mountain customs."

According to June Brown, "Aunt Cecil had a bit of a temper, but it took a lot to really make her lose it. You should have talked with Colonel Stephans! They went around a few times. When she decided to do something, she went ahead with it and then called him up to tell him about it. *It was easier to get forgiveness than permission, I guess.* But Colonel Stephans supported her wholeheartedly, and he won a lot of battles for her. He really went to bat for her a lot of times. I remember once some auditors came to do the books. They questioned some records that she probably should have asked for permission and/or guidance on – but you can't argue with success. She did a great service for the mountain area, so you can't fault her, really."

To Brigadier James Henry, "Cecil was a woman of vision, because in those days these mountains were wild and wooly – with moonshiners and all sorts of characters. She came in here and she told the people how it was. They knew her, you see, so she could say to them, 'I've come back here to preach Jesus to you!'"

Florence Wall said, "Cecil and her whole family were involved in the Mountain Mission work. We appreciated the staff gatherings she held with us because we needed to know what was going on. At our initial meeting, we received our work assignments for the first six weeks, but we knew those assignments could change at any time. We needed her guidance. It was a whole new ballgame, as far as I was concerned. We no longer had any of the conveniences we were used to – running water, indoor facilities, or electricity. To me, it was a big adventure."

Mildred Kirby said, "I saw her lose her temper on occasion, although she wasn't violent. She didn't have a lot of patience with people who didn't catch on to what she wanted. If she gave you instructions, she expected you to remember them and to do exactly what she said. If you thought you could do it better your way, think again. Don't do it. Instead, you'd better do it her way."

Lieutenant Florence Wall leads a sing-along.

Chapter 17

The Final Journey

Cecil and Thelma Colton made great strides in the mission during the seven years that they worked together. At its zenith, no less than ten corps and outposts were up and running, or at least in the planning stages: Maple Springs Citadel, Shelton Laurel, Cold Springs, Max Patch, Sleepy Valley, Bonnie Hill, Little Creek, Big Bend, White Oak and Spring Creek. Other missions came and went – Timber Ridge, Fines Creek, Hurricane Creek, Poplar Gap, and a few others whose names have faded away.

By the time sickness forced an early retirement, Cecil estimated that she had worn out 18 cars, several horses, and dozens of pairs of shoes and boots. It was not uncommon for her to travel 15 miles over rough roads, rain or shine, to hold a Sunday service, or to drive a sick person 25 miles to the hospital. In later years she drove in a jeep over the state and county roads that led to most of her missions. In 1946, she had a five-year old car with 100,000 miles on it. Cecil entered situations where even the bravest men proceeded with caution. She had a message to carry. She knew she was right, and nothing else mattered. "No frontiers in America? No modern pioneers? Just spend a day with me," she once said.

FAVORITE EVENTS

She took particular pride in two annual Army events – the Singing Convention (usually held in August) and the celebration of the Christmas holidays.

The first Singing Convention, also known as "Singing On The Mountain," was held in 1936 with 250 people in attendance. The twentieth observance of this event coincided with Cecil's retirement in June 1956. By that time annual attendance had soared to over 3,000 people from 16 states.

Christmas held a special place in Cecil's heart. Within a short couple of years, children across the Smoky Mountains went from barely any observance to anticipating a visit from the Santa's helper who wore blue. At least eight Christmas parties dotted the Mountain Mission, celebrating the good news of Christ's birth in the remotest coves and hollows. Most of the children's gifts came from cash and in-kind donations received from all over the South.

PROMOTING THE MISSION

During Christmas of 1946, Cecil's popularity hit an all-time high. An estimated 10 million listeners heard the CBS radio program, *"We The People,"* promote the work of The Salvation Army all over America. After Cecil spoke from a microphone at Asheville's radio station WWNC, requests for more information on the Mountain Mission flooded CBS offices in New York City and Army posts around the country.

Even the work's moniker took its own shape. When the opening of the first corps received official sanction in 1936, the divisional commander suggested to Atlanta headquarters that the proposed series of missions be named either the Salvation Army Circle Corps or the Mountain District. The work eventually became known by the now familiar "Mountain Mission."

VACANCY

In the mid-1940s, when Adjutant Brown became Major Brown, she suffered a devastating blow after Thelma Colton, her trusted aide, answered a call to ministry in another denomination. The rumors of a rift between Thelma and Cecil had no apparent basis in fact. Without her chief right hand, however, Cecil's workload more or less doubled. A series of single women lieutenants ensued in the remaining years of her ministry, and although she relied heavily on them, she missed the natural rapport she had enjoyed with Thelma.

As in the past, Cecil's tough style of leadership continued to evoke both positive and negative sentiment from her subordinates. Incoming lieutenants had a hard act to follow, and some began to resent Cecil and her methods. A few called her a bully who was impossible to please. One assistant still bears scars from her relationship with Cecil, and another found her impossible to work with after she received the Order of the Founder in 1947. In sharp contrast, however, a third lieutenant noted that the award meant nothing to her and that "she was very humble about it."

During Christmas of 1950 she lacked any "official" help, although soldiers and family members stepped in and ably filled the void. Even the children who lived in the Army's home worked every day and many nights to be sure that each young person on the list received a present.

HER FINAL YEARS

Lieutenant Colonel Gus Stephans, divisional commander for the Carolinas, recognized the importance of the Mountain Mission and gave Cecil as much, if not more support, than she had received from past Army leaders. Perhaps because of her slowly deteriorating health, she seemed more stressed, more agitated and more demanding. She still wore her hair in a bun to comply with Army regulations, and the hairpins continuously left sores on the back of her neck. A growth emerged, which could have been a precursor to the stomach cancer that finally took her life.

Despite his overall support, Lieutenant Colonel Stephans sometimes had trouble tolerating her general irritability. On several occasions, he was overheard pacing in his Charlotte office, wringing his hands and lamenting, "I just don't know what I'm going to do with that woman!"

GLENNA AND JEAN

Once Thelma had left the mountains, Cecil continually searched for capable single women to replace her close friend and her trusted colleague. Two women who came closest to meeting her standards were Glenna West and Jean Frese. Glenna, the only native of the Mountain Mission who became a Salvation Army officer, served in one corps appointment and then gladly returned home to work with Cecil in the mountains. Jean and Cecil grew so close that Cecil considered adopting her as a daughter, but the process was never finalized. Jean, who assisted in the mountain work long after Cecil died, became an officer and served in many other appointments. Later she came back to the Mountain Mission and worked there until the mid-1980s.

Now retired, Jean lives in her modest home on the Mountain Mission grounds and across from the present site of the Shelton Laurel Corps. Her collection of Cecil Brown memorabilia is impressive. She even owns a piece of furniture that had been hewn by Cecil's brother. She hopes to erect a memorial to Cecil and the Army's Mountain Mission some day.

By the early 1950s the heyday of the Mountain Mission seemed to have passed. The outside world had invaded the quiet mountains. Paved roads and bridges made travel to the big cities possible, and electricity, accompanied by television, brought civilization into the mountain cabins. Cecil Brown and her sisters helped to bring about overdue modernization when they petitioned the governor of North Carolina, William K. Scott, to provide public services that were taken for granted elsewhere in the United States. Putting her able networking skills to use, Cecil found an important ally in John D. Langston of Goldsboro, N.C., who was the father of Brigadier Dorothy Langston. He convinced the electrical companies to lay the first power lines in the remotest parts of the Great Smoky Mountains.

"This hinterland is beginning to crack its shell," the *Mountain Circle News* announced in February 1950. "I tell you, it makes you feel mighty proud to live in a land where you can see some progress at every turn of the road." At long last, residents were living in remodeled homes with running water, refrigerators, washing machines and telephones. They reaped the benefits of modern farm equipment, transportation, and communication. Young people began to leave to seek a better life. The need for a Cecil Brown had changed dramatically.

It was a bittersweet situation. By this time, Major Cecil Brown's success as a missionary had made her into an institution. She had lifted her people to new heights within the span of two decades.

The record shows that more people accepted Christianity in the privacy of their own homes than at the altars of Army chapels. An unrecorded number were saved as they knelt with Cecil on the dirt floor of many a mountain cabin. Therein lies the secret of her success.

Cecil was a mission builder. If at least five families lived within walking distance, no other spiritual support existed, and she had at least a one-room cabin available, she would open another corps.

A LOCAL HERO

Cecil's retirement at the age of 49 drew massive crowds, and state and county police had to maintain crowd control. A "who's who" of Salvation Army dignitaries came to honor her, including her territorial commander and Commissioner William J. Dray, along with field secretary Lieutenant Colonel Robert Rose and all of the divisional headquarters staff.

On June 10, 1956, the entire Sunday was set aside for three meetings at Max Patch. In the morning, Thelma Colton led the Singing Convention, introducing a message and special singers. The retirement ceremony, conducted by Commissioner Dray, took place in the afternoon. Lattie Henderson led the decoration of the Hurricane View Cemetery, which was an annual rite and part of each Singing Convention.

The evening program featured a movie, *The Shepherdess of the Hills*, using footage shot by Colonel Stephans and narration written by Major Ivy Waterworth. Cecil's actual retirement took effect on July 8, 1956.

In her remarks following the ceremony, she said that she looked forward to a less demanding, simpler life. She would return to the same house where she had grown up a half-century earlier. The house had become vacant after her family moved out, about 30 years before the retired "Maid of the Mountains" moved back in.

Ironically, just as the hollows of western North Carolina had finally progressed into the twentieth century, Cecil relished the prospect of continuing her pioneer lifestyle just off the new Pigeon River Road. "This will be primitive living," she said. "I will be one mile from the nearest neighbor, six miles from the nearest mailbox, and 30 miles from town. There will be no electricity or modern conveniences – I will carry my water from the spring, cook on a wood stove, and get out the old oil lamps. But I'm going to enjoy every minute of it."

A LIFE-LONG DREAM

Fulfilling a longtime dream, she took an ambitious two-month camping trip to Alaska with Blanche Lowe and two other children from the Mountain Ministry. Cecil's brother had attached a small camper on the back of a truck and installed a gas burner for her. Along the highway, then an unpaved dirt road, the group enjoyed glimpses of bear, moose and other wild game. Although local authorities advised motorists not to drive after a rain for safety reasons, Cecil never wanted to stop long enough to wait for the road to dry. Once the truck slid off the road, and some lumberjacks had to tow it with ropes and chains.

Soon after the trip to Alaska, Cecil began to weaken seriously. On June 24, 1957, she had surgery in Asheville in an effort to curtail her cancer. A letter from Blanche following the operation described her sanguine attitude toward being bedridden with a colostomy. "She is in good spirits, and she says she will lick this problem the same as she has had to lick every other problem." As the end neared, she became reclusive. Cecil's mother and Blanche checked on her on the morning of December 4, 1958, and found that she had died during the night. "When Granny Brown and I looked in on her we thought she was simply asleep, but after a while we looked closer and realized that Cecil was gone," Blanche said.

James Henry received a call shortly afterward from one of Cecil's family members: "Captain, sister has just gone to Glory. We're going to have the funeral tomorrow at one o'clock. Would you see that the chapel is warmed?"

Prior to her death, she had given instructions to the funeral home concerning preparation of her body. "I want my hair arranged just like I have worn it since I was 16 years old and switched from pigtails to the Salvation Army 'bun' style. I would request that the funeral director not put any makeup on me. On the resurrection morning I would like to know that the Lord will recognize me, and He wouldn't if I was all painted up," she said wryly more than once.

The funeral service took place at the Maple Springs Citadel Corps, with attendance exceeding the retirement service turnout two years earlier. Army dignitaries included Colonel Gus Stephans from territorial headquarters, and Mrs. Commissioner Ernest Pugmire from national headquarters in New York City.

Reverend Pete Hicks, a friend of the Brown family from Canton, North Carolina, read Psalm 23, which had been Major Brown's favorite scripture. In his eulogy he called Cecil "a missionary of the highest type – duty-bound to give her life for others."

As Reverend Hicks harkened back through the years he had known her, he shared two incidents from her ministry. There was a time at Big Bend that a child lay dying, and the family sent a runner up the mountain for Cecil. She hurried down the mountain and waded through a river to reach the sick child's home. The weather was so cold that Cecil's wet clothes froze and became stiff. When she arrived at the cabin, she took the child to Waynesville. The doctors, who were unable to help, moved her to Asheville, where the toddler died. Then Cecil brought the child back to Big Bend, prepared the body for burial and conducted the funeral service.

Reverend Hicks also cited the time Cecil had cleared out the bootleggers from one community. He remembered her as an organizer, a builder, a leader, and someone who taught little children how to pray. "Cecil will long be remembered, greatly loved and appreciated. May her passing be the means of helping us to carry on what she began in North Carolina," he said in closing.

The Great Smoky Mountains are named because of a fog that often hovers over random parts of the mountain chain. On the day of Cecil Brown's funeral, it permeated the Maple Springs mountain. As the casket was taken across the road to the Hurricane View Cemetery, the fog noticeably lifted for the committal service to reveal a breathtaking view of mountain peaks rising in the distance.

"Harry and I were corps officers in Florida when we heard that Major Brown had died," Mildred Kirby said. "We were in Bradenton when we read about it in the paper. That's how we found out. Imagine that she was so well-known that a newspaper in Florida carried the news of her death."

"Long after Aunt Cecil was gone, I would often catch myself picking up the phone to call her to see how she was doing," June Brown said. "It was so hard for me, because my mother was taken by cancer, and Aunt Cecil became a mother to me."

"I guess the saddest thing about her passing is the fact that she seemed to be one of those people that you think is going to be around forever," Dean Self said. "I remember going home after she had died, and I couldn't stop crying. Here I am, a grown woman with children of my own – but it was so sad. It was the end of an era for me, because she wouldn't be around anymore."

On the twenty-second anniversary of her appointment to the mountains, Cecil had given a rare glimpse into her soul in her newsletter, *Mountain Life:* "I had nothing more in mind than to hide away in the city and carry on the old Methodist circuit riders' work that died out with the horse and buggy. Had I known what my hands would do during twenty-two years of hard work, I may have been frightened. But twenty-two years ago I wasn't afraid of anything. So I set to work – I haven't let one blade of grass grow under my feet, and today I am happy to look over the ground I covered and thank the Heavenly Father for His promises to me.

"I shall never forget standing on top of the mountain here and looking over the vast mountain ranges, and saying to Him, 'The Mountains shall be Thine!'"

Captain James Henry (left) at Cecil's retirement

Epilogue

Cecil Brown came to help the mountaineers of North Carolina when they needed her most, and she left a cherished mark on their lives. As she raised them to new spiritual and social heights, the civilized world was making advances as well. World War II brought an end to the Great Depression, and the golden age of television gradually invaded the homes in the Great Smoky Mountains. Slowly but surely, people moved out of the area. The high tide of Cecil's domain came in the 1940s and then ebbed. By the time she retired and died in the late 1950's, the need for her services had largely ended.

Brigadier James Henry succeeded Cecil after she retired in 1956. "Big Jim," a mountain native and a legend in his own right, was one of only a few people who could have followed her and built on the foundation she had laid for 20 years. Still, he found the going tough during his tenure, mainly because her image had been indelibly etched on the hearts of the mountain people. He eventually made inroads as well as a place for himself in the Mountain Mission lore.

Today, the Salvation Army still works in western North Carolina, but little remains of the vision that Cecil brought with her there 70 years ago. As the descendants of her congregations have moved to larger towns in more prosperous counties, one by one the Army has been forced to close the corps she pioneered. Today, Army leadership continues to explore how best to meet the spiritual and social needs of a shifting society.

Major Vern Jewett, the current divisional commander for the Army's work in North and South Carolina, believes that Cecil Brown's trailblazing spirit can best be memorialized by exploring how the Salvation Army can continue to be of service in communities throughout the Smokies.

"Many changes have taken place in the more than half century which has lapsed since the height of Major Cecil Brown's ministry. The Salvation Army continues to serve in some of the same small mountain communities with corps in Waynesville, Shelton-Laurel, Sleepy Valley and Bonnie Hill," he said. "The mountains have become more accessible as roads and bridges have reached into previously isolated communities. Recent generations of young men and women have migrated into the larger communities seeking employment in Franklin, Sylva and Murphy along with other growing communities. Many counties that previously qualified as impoverished now are actually becoming affluent. Western North Carolina is becoming a haven for retirement communities and the population is aging rapidly. The Salvation Army can be counted on to respond to the lingering needs of Major Cecil Brown's beloved mountain residents and communities as well as to face the new challenges emerging in the twenty-first century."

Cecil fishing on Pigeon River

The Author

Major Frank Duracher is a native of New Orleans, La., and has served as a Salvation Army officer since 1975. He graduated magna cum laude with a B.A. from Seton Hall University and summa cum laude with a M.A. from Jacksonville State University. He presently serves as assistant editor of the Army's territorial publication, *Southern Spirit*, and has a regular newspaper column called *Rays of Hope*. He writes devotionals for *Reflecting God – Devotionals for Holy Living*, published in all four USA Territories, as well as *Heartbeat*, a radio program heard on more than 1,500 stations around the world.

Crest  Books

Salvation Army National Publications

Crest Books, a division of The Salvation Army's National Publications department, was established in 1997 so contemporary Salvationist voices could be captured and bound in enduring form for future generations, to serve as witnesses to the continuing force and mission of the Army.

Shaw Clifton, *Never the Same Again: Encouragement for new and not–so–new Christians*, 1997

Compilation, *Christmas Through the Years: A War Cry Treasury*, 1997

William Francis, *Celebrate the Feasts of the Lord: The Christian Heritage of the Sacred Jewish Festivals*, 1998

Marlene Chase, *Pictures from the Word*, 1998

Joe Noland, *A Little Greatness*, 1998

Lyell M. Rader, *Romance & Dynamite: Essays on Science & the Nature of Faith*, 1998

Shaw Clifton, *Who Are These Salvationists? An Analysis for the 21st Century*, 1999

Compilation, *Easter Through the Years: A War Cry Treasury*, 1999

Terry Camsey, *Slightly Off Center! Growth Principles to Thaw Frozen Paradigms*, 2000

Philip Needham, *He Who Laughed First: Delighting in a Holy God*, (in collaboration with Beacon Hill Press, Kansas City), 2000

Henry Gariepy, ed., *A Salvationist Treasury: 365 Devotional Meditations from the Classics to the Contemporary*, 2000

Marlene Chase, *Our God Comes: And Will Not Be Silent*, 2001

A. Kenneth Wilson, *Fractured Parables: And Other Tales to Lighten the Heart and Quicken the Spirit*, 2001

Carroll Ferguson Hunt, *If Two Shall Agree* (in collaboration with Beacon Hill Press, Kansas City), 2001

John C. Izzard, *Pen of Flame: The Life and Poetry of Catherine Baird*, 2002

Henry Gariepy, *Andy Miller: A Legend and a Legacy*, 2002

Compilation, *A Word in Season: A Collection of Short Stories*, 2002

R. David Rightmire, *Sanctified Sanity: The Life and Teaching of Samuel Logan Brengle*, 2003

Chick Yuill, *Leadership on the Axis of Change*, 2003

Compilation, *Living Portraits Speaking Still: A Collection of Bible Studies*, 2004

A. Kenneth Wilson, *The First Dysfunctional Family: A Modern Guide to the Book of Genesis*, 2004

Allen Satterlee, *Turning Points: How The Salvation Army Found a Different Path*, 2004

David Laeger, *Shadow and Substance: The Tabernacle of the Human Heart*, 2005

Check Yee, *Good Morning China*, 2005

Marlene Chase, *Beside Still Waters: Great Prayers of the Bible for Today*, 2005

Roger J. Green, *The Life & Ministry of William Booth* (in collaboration with Abingdon Press, Nashville), 2006

Norman H. Murdoch, *Soldiers of the Cross: Susie Swift and David Lamb, 2006*

Henry Gariepy, *Israel L. Gaither: Man with a Mission*, 2006

R.G. Moyles (ed.), *I Knew William Booth, 2007*

John Larsson, *Saying Yes to Life*, 2007

All titles by Crest Books can be purchased through your nearest

Salvation Army Supplies and Purchasing department:

ATLANTA, GA—(800) 786–7372
DES PLAINES, IL—(800) 937–8896
LONG BEACH, CA—(800) 937–8896
WEST NYACK, NY—(888) 488–4882